Texas Assessment Preparation

Grade 5

Texas JOURNEYS

Texas WRITE SOURCE

 HOUGHTON MIFFLIN HARCOURT

Contents

How To Use This Book

Texas Assessment Preparation is designed to help you practice for the Texas reading and writing assessments. This book includes sections on Reading, Writing, Revising, and Editing.

- **Reading**   This section includes passages of literature in a variety of literary genres. A **genre** is a type of literature, such as fiction, expository nonfiction, or poetry. Helpful **Tips** guide you as you read the passages and answer the questions about them.

- **Writing**   This section provides prompts for writing one-page personal narratives and one-page expository compositions. Models of student writing show you what to do (and not do) in order to write well.

- **Revising and Editing**   These sections provide practice for improving your writing before creating a final draft.

Get Credit for Your Answers

- **Multiple-Choice Questions**   Your teacher will give you an Answer Document before you begin your work. Fill in each correct answer bubble completely. Check your work. Be sure you have not skipped an item or filled in more than one bubble for an item.

- **Writing Prompts**   You may use a separate sheet of paper to write a first draft for each writing prompt. Always write as clearly as possible. Be sure that your final draft is no more than one page long.

Read the Signs

As you work through this book, you will see the signs and symbols below. Be sure you understand what they mean and what to do when you see them.

Read this selection.	Words in a box give directions. Read them carefully to make sure you understand what to do.
In paragraph 10, the word <u>genre</u> means —	Pay attention to underlined words in a passage. These words will appear later in questions about the passage.
What is the **BEST** way to revise sentence 7?	Boldfaced, capitalized words in test items help you eliminate weaker answer choices.
GO ON ➤	This symbol tells you to go on to the next page.
STOP	This symbol means that you should put your pencil down.

Texas Assessment
Practice

Fiction

Genre Overview

Fiction refers to a story that is made up. **Realistic fiction** is a made-up story that could take place in real life. Sometimes, a story will include other types of text, such as advertisements, e-mail correspondence, or informational flyers that are written from a particular point of view. This additional text can make the story seem more realistic. It can also introduce new information into the narrative.

In every fiction story, there is at least one **character**, at least one **setting**, and a **plot**. These elements are organized into a **story structure**. The author puts them together in a way that will best tell the story. When you **summarize** a story, you retell the main events of the narrative. You leave out details that do not advance the story significantly.

As you read a fiction story, identify the **characters**. Ask yourself, *Who is this story mostly about?* That person is the **main character**. Often, you will have to make an inference about why characters act and speak as they do. It may help to **paraphrase** information from the story. When you paraphrase, you restate what happens, using your own words.

The **setting** is the place and time in which the story happens. To identify the setting, ask yourself, *Where and when does this story take place?*

The **plot** is what happens in a story. The plot is made up of a series of events. The **conflict**, or **problem**, is introduced at the beginning of the story. As we read, we look for the events that move the action along. The **resolution**, or **solution** to the problem, is how the problem is solved.

The **narrator** is the person who tells, or narrates, a story. When planning a work of fiction, the author must decide who that narrator will be.

When a character tells a story, he or she is called a **first-person** narrator. A first-person narrator uses the words *I* and *we* to tell the story.

When the narrator is not a character in the story, he or she is called a **third-person** narrator. A third-person narrator tells the story using words such as *he, she,* and *they*. Third-person **omniscient** narrators know what all the characters in a story are thinking and feeling. Third-person **limited** narrators reveal only the thoughts and feelings of a story's main character.

Fiction

> **Read this selection. Then answer the questions that follow it.**
> **Fill in the circle of the correct answer on your answer document.**

The Case of the Glowing Glove

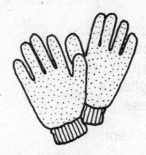

1   "Alex Lopez," the dark-haired boy said, shaking the trembling hand of his newest client. "And this," he continued with a nod at Ben Douglas, "is my able assistant."

2   The new client was as nervous as a cat at a dog show. He obviously hadn't had a good night's sleep. The dark circles under his rapidly blinking eyes told the story. Silently, he held out a scrap of paper. The advertisement said:

3
> We are pleased to announce the official opening of our detective agency, Lopez & Douglas. No job is too big or too small for us, and our work is free of charge. Master detective Alex Lopez has a 100% success rate in solving cases. All information will be kept strictly private. You can contact us by phone at 972-555-8986 or drop your letter of inquiry into the mailbox at 308 Bluebell Lane. Mr. Lopez or his assistant Mr. Douglas will handle your call personally.

4   "Ah, that's how you found us. Come with me," the young detective said, leading the visitor to a tiny but practical office. It wasn't much, this closet under the stairs in the basement, but it worked for Alex. He could, however, see that this nervous and sleepy client was not impressed.

5   "It's okay, " Ben assured the visitor. "Alex is the best detective in Harris Canyon Middle School."

6   "I'm sorry," said the client, "but I didn't sleep much last night. I just couldn't take my eyes off it."

7   "It?" Ben asked, pencil paused midair.

8   "This!" The client, Marshall Turner, seventh grader at Harris Canyon, held before them a glove—an ordinary work glove, like the kind worn to clean the garage. It was stiff and had the cracked appearance of an elephant's hide. Otherwise, it seemed ordinary and harmless.

9   Ben and Alex glanced at each other. "A glove kept you awake?" Alex asked.

10   Marshall reached up and flipped off the light switch. The closet, or rather, the office, was instantly dark, yet something glowed. It was the glove!

11   This was certainly a strange development. Alex wished that Marshall hadn't removed the glove from where he found it, but then, Marshall lacked the wisdom of an experienced detective. A visit to the client's house was in order, as Alex and Ben needed to view the glove as Marshall had seen it the night before.

12   Fortunately, Marshall lived close by in an old house. As the boys walked up the creaky stairs to Marshall's attic bedroom, Alex felt something watching them.

13   Once in the attic, Alex surveyed the ancient rafters of the house. He asked, "Precisely where was the glowing glove?"

14   Marshall pointed to the open closet door. "I went to bed, as usual, first turning out the lamp by my bed. There was no moon last night, so the room was completely dark. I was just about to shut my eyes," he gulped, "when I saw fingers curled around the edge of the closet door, looking as though they were just about to pull the door closed from the inside. I stared and stared, but the fingers never moved. I must have fallen asleep at some point, and when I woke up, sunlight flooded the room. I leaped out of bed and ran to the closet. There was this glove, an ordinary gray glove, lying on the rug."

> **Tip**
>
> Think about what the client wants Alex and Ben to notice about the glove. Why is this ordinary piece of clothing so alarming to Marshall?

GO ON

Name _____ Date _____

TEKS 5.6A, 5.6B, 5.6C, 5.14C, RC-5(D), RC-5(E)

15   Marshall sank onto his bed, exhausted by his tale of terror. Ben scribbled something in his notebook, and Alex once again had the alarming sense that a pair of eyes was trained on them.

16   "Gladys!" Marshall suddenly shouted. Ben jumped, while Alex turned in time to see a hound dog snatch the glove from Marshall with its flashing white teeth and bound toward the stairs.

17   When they finally caught up with Gladys out in the yard, she was wagging her tail and chewing on a rubber bone. Beside her was the mate of the mysterious glove, along with an old bicycle that appeared freshly painted. A tall young man whom Alex took to be one of Marshall's older brothers was also present. "Sir," Alex said respectfully, "what do you know about this extraordinary glove, the subject of our mystery?"

> **Tip**
>
> Notice Gladys's role in the story. Think about her actions and how they are tied to future plot events.

18   "I was painting my bike yesterday when Gladys decided that she wanted to romp. I took off my gloves to play with a stick, but she fetched one of my gloves instead." Marshall's brother patted the dog's head fondly. "So she left it with you, eh, little brother?"

19   Alex thought hard. The mystery of how the glove came to be in the attic was solved, but why did the glove glow? Just then, the bike caught the detective's eye. It was almost the same shade as the glove. Suddenly, the facts clicked into place.

20   "Luminescent paint!" Alex exclaimed. "You painted your bike with paint that glows in the dark!"

21   "Yes," the young man answered. "I want to be able to ride home safely from afternoon basketball practice."

22   Ben nodded his head while Marshall looked at Alex, completely confused. Alex held up the glove, explaining that the material was coated with the luminescent paint from the bike. "That's why it glowed in the dark," Alex announced triumphantly.

23   Marshall sighed. "Whew! Thanks for solving the mystery, Alex. Now, I'm going to take a nap!"

1 What is Marshall's problem in the story?

   A He must find the missing glove for his brother.

   B He doesn't trust Alex and Ben to solve the mystery.

   C He is frightened by a glove that glows in the dark.

   D He must keep his dog away from the painted bike.

TEKS 5.6B

2 Refer to the advertisement in the story. The writer of the advertisement believes that—

   F the new agency is not likely to attract many clients

   G clients do not care if their problems remain a secret

   H the agency will be successful in solving all of its cases

   J clients usually have problems of a very serious nature

TEKS 5.14C

Tip
Think about the attitude and viewpoint of the character who wrote the advertisement. Does he believe the new agency will attract clients and solve cases?

3 Seeing what happens from the viewpoint of a narrator outside the story helps the reader understand—

   A what Marshall thinks of Alex and Ben

   B which character may be guilty

   C how Alex and Ben opened their detective agency

   D what all of the characters are thinking and feeling

TEKS 5.6C

4 Look at the story map below.

Beginning	Middle	Ending
The detectives take on the case.	Marshall sinks down on his bed.	

Which detail belongs in the blank box?

F Marshall tells Ben and Alex his problem.

G The boys climb the creaking stairs.

H Marshall holds out a scrap of paper.

J Gladys carries the glove to the yard.

TEKS 5.6A

Tip
Look for the event that gives Alex an important clue to the mystery.

5 The reader can tell that Alex is—

A easily confused

B very confident

C somewhat rude

D slightly nervous

TEKS RC-5(D)

6 Which of the following is the best summary of this story?

F Alex and Ben like to solve mysteries. One day, Marshall comes to Alex's office with a case. He wants to know what makes an ordinary glove suddenly start glowing. All three boys visit Marshall's house in search of clues to the mystery.

G One day, Alex and Ben receive a visitor. Marshall has lost sleep because a glove in his room started to glow in the middle of the night. Marshall is tired and very worried. He hopes Alex can solve this mystery for him.

H One afternoon, Marshall's brother decides to paint his bike with glowing paint. That night, a glove begins to glow mysteriously. Marshall has no idea what has caused this to happen. He wants Alex and Ben to help him solve this mystery.

J Marshall loses sleep when a glove in his room begins to glow. He takes his case to Alex and Ben, who visit Marshall's home in search of clues. When Alex compares a freshly painted bike to the glowing glove, he solves the mystery.

TEKS RC-5(E)

13

Name _____ Date _____

Literary Nonfiction

Genre Overview

Literary nonfiction is a form of writing that uses elements of fiction to tell a true story about a **subject**.

An **autobiography** is a type of literary nonfiction that tells the story of a person's life, written by that person. In writing an autobiography, an author tells the most meaningful events in his or her life. The author might also share lessons he or she has learned over time.

A **biography** is literary nonfiction that tells the story of a person's life, written by someone else. A good biography creates a full, accurate picture of its subject. It also presents the writer's understanding and opinion about the subject.

When telling the story of a person's life, the author usually presents events in **chronological order**, or the time order in which they happened. Readers can use their own words to **summarize** or **paraphrase** the sequence of events if it becomes difficult to follow. Sometimes the author will make the meaning of important events clear for the reader. Other times, readers will have to figure things out on their own by **making inferences** or **drawing conclusions** based on evidence in the text.

Literary nonfiction commonly includes **academic language**, such as special words used in science and social studies writing. Some of these words might include **Latin and Greek roots and affixes**. Use what you know about Latin and Greek word parts to help you understand the meaning of these words.

Grade 5: Literary Nonfiction

Literary Nonfiction

> **Read this selection. Then answer the questions that follow it.**
> **Fill in the circle of the correct answer on your answer document.**

Abigail Adams: A Woman Ahead of Her Time

1   Abigail Adams lived at a time when women could not vote, hold office, or attend college. In the late 1700s, many people believed that a formal education was actually a disadvantage for a woman. They thought it would make a woman think she knew as much as her husband!

Tip
Notice that this information introduces the reader to a woman who was unusual for her place and time.

2   Abigail Adams didn't see things that way. She supported women's rights, believing that women and men should be treated as equals. In 1776, her husband, John Adams, was in Philadelphia to help write the Declaration of Independence. Back home in Massachusetts, Abigail Adams wrote a letter to her husband, urging him to "remember the ladies" as men wrote the country's new laws.

3   Over the years, Abigail Adams wrote many letters to her husband. During the Revolutionary War, while John Adams was a delegate to the Continental Congress in Philadelphia, she wrote to inform him about the activities of British troops in the Boston area. In addition to sending details, her letters included opinions about what was unfair about society at the time. She regretted her

Grade 5: Literary Nonfiction

lack of schooling. Because of this, she insisted that her daughter receive a well-rounded education.

4   Abigail Adams made a point of speaking up about what she believed in. She had to admit, though, that being outspoken could cause problems. When her husband ran for President of the United States in 1796, Abigail Adams worried about becoming First Lady. As the President's wife, she would sometimes have to keep her opinions to herself. She told her husband, "I must impose a silence upon myself when I long to talk." She was not sure she could do that. In 1797, John Adams was elected President. Soon after the election, Abigail Adams discovered the power of the press.

5   The newspapers reported what the First Lady said and did. They always seemed to find something to criticize. Some said she spent too much money. Others accused her of being cheap. The most hurtful charge was that she influenced her husband's political decisions. After three years of being misquoted and misunderstood, Abigail Adams learned to choose her words with care. When she and her husband moved to Washington, D.C., the new capital city, she praised the newly built President's house, later known as the White House. She stated that it was "built for ages to come," and she kept herself from pointing out that it was not quite ready to live in!

6   In fact, the house was still being built when John Adams moved in, and the rooms were not finished. It was cold, dark, and damp, even with fires burning in all thirteen of its fireplaces. Abigail Adams refused to hang her laundry outside the house for everyone to see, so she ended up hanging a clothesline across the conference room. After all, she explained to her sister, in its unfinished condition the room was good for little else! She also thought the house was much too big. She remarked that it would take thirty servants to run such a "castle of a house," and she could afford only thirteen.

Tip

Look for details that show what Abigail Adams felt about living in the White House.

GO ON ▶

Name _____ Date _____

TEKS 5.2A, 5.7,
RC-5(D), RC-5(E)

7   What bothered Abigail Adams most about life in
Washington, D.C., was the widespread use of slave
labor. She had always believed that slavery was wrong.
On this subject, she did speak her mind. She had
learned to give in on minor matters, but she would never
compromise on important issues. Abigail Adams was a
woman who knew her mind. She was also a woman who
was ahead of her time.

1 Look at the chart below.

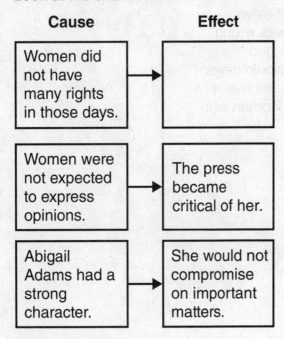

Which sentence belongs in the empty box?

A Women like Abigail Adams could not vote or attend college.

B Many Washington leaders admired Abigail Adams.

C Abigail Adams sometimes spent too much money.

D Many women followed the example set by Abigail Adams.

TEKS 5.7

2 Which best describes how the author presents major events in the life of Abigail Adams?

F By including different opinions about her life

G By posing questions about her life and then answering those questions

H By describing the events in chronological order

J By comparing the events to the lives of other women during that time period

TEKS 5.7

Tip
Check the passage against each of the choices. Which choice can be supported by the text?

3 Why did Abigail Adams write so many letters during her lifetime?

A She did not have any interesting hobbies.

B She wanted to get her letters published.

C She was often apart from her husband.

D She wanted to tell friends about Washington.

TEKS RC-5(D)

Tip
Think about John Adams's responsibilities during his life of service to his country. What did his work mean for his family?

Name _____ Date _____

4 In paragraph 5, the word <u>misquoted</u> means—

F quoted often

G quoted correctly

H never quoted

J not quoted correctly

TEKS 5.2A

5 In paragraph 7, why does the author say that Abigail Adams was "ahead of her time"?

A She thought and acted like a modern woman.

B She was a great leader in Washington circles.

C She was as educated as the women of today.

D She was not patient enough to deal with others.

TEKS RC-5(D)

6 Which of the following is the best summary of paragraphs 2 and 3?

F Abigail Adams was a supporter of equal rights for women and a sharp critic of social wrongs. Although she felt awkward about her writing, her letters were full of important facts about the Revolutionary War and ideas for improving American society.

G Abigail Adams never went to college. Her letters were full of spelling mistakes, but she kept on writing. She told her husband John Adams to "remember the ladies." She wanted her daughter to get a good education.

H Abigail Adams lived in Boston at the time of the Revolutionary War. She wrote her husband letters about what the British troops did. She believed men and women should be treated as equals.

J Abigail Adams worried about her spelling and grammar but wrote many letters expressing her ideas. Some of her letters were about the war. She made sure that her daughter received a good education because she never had that opportunity.

TEKS RC-5(E)

Grade 5 Literary fiction

Name _____ Date _____

Expository Text

Genre Overview

Expository text gives facts and information about a topic. This kind of text usually states a **main idea**, or central idea, about the topic and provides **details** and **facts** to support it. As you read, notice that the author may also express **opinions**, or personal beliefs, about the topic. Consider both the facts and opinions in the selection to **draw conclusions**, or come to a reasoned judgment, about what you have read.

Expository text is organized in a particular pattern, such as **comparison-contrast, sequential order, logical order**, or **cause-and-effect**. A text may have more than one organizational pattern. For example, the writer may present most of the ideas in a selection in the **order** in which they happened but organize a particular paragraph with a cause-and-effect structure to show *why* something happened. Understanding the way a selection is organized can help you to **make connections** between ideas and information in a text.

Expository writing may include **procedural text**, which includes directions or steps in a process. The writer will organize the steps in a process in a specific sequence. A reader can then follow the steps to complete a task or solve a problem.

Expository text may make use of **text features** such as bold print, headings, captions, key words, and italics. These features can help you find information. For example, a bold word might point out an important idea. It might also tell you that a definition or example of the word follows. Expository writing can also include **graphic features**, such as maps, charts, illustrations, and diagrams. These features can add information to the selection or present facts in a form that is easy to see.

> **Read this selection. Then answer the questions that follow it.**
> **Fill in the circle of the correct answer on your answer document.**

The Wonderful Wheel of Mr. Ferris

1   Almost every amusement park or town fair has a
Ferris wheel. Ferris wheels are so common that people
do not think much about how the ride came to be so
popular or how it got its name.

A Wonderful Invention

2   The Ferris wheel is named for its inventor, George
Washington Gale Ferris. Ferris designed the new ride to
be part of the World's Fair that was called the Columbian
Exposition. This fair, held in Chicago in 1893, celebrated
the 400th anniversary of the landing of Columbus in
America.

> **Tip**
>
> Look for facts about the Ferris
> wheel and the World's Fair.

The 1893 World's Fair

3   The Columbian Exposition introduced people to
cultures from around the world. It also showed them new
inventions and discoveries. In the 1890s, many people
had not seen what electricity could do. In fact, some
people feared it. The 1893 World's Fair used electric lights
in ways that people had not seen before. The buildings
were lit with many lights at night. The Ferris wheel

> **Tip**
>
> Notice what people at the
> World's Fair learned about the
> uses of electricity.

21

gleamed brightly, too. It was lit with thousands of electric lights.

Ferris's Wheel

4   The amazing ride stood 264 feet high. Its giant wheel spun on a steel axle. At the time, that axle was the largest piece of forged steel ever made. The cars where people sat were much larger than the ones we ride in today. There were 36 cars on the wheel. Each car could hold as many as 60 people. More than 2,000 people could ride at one time.

Tip

Look for supporting details that explain why the Ferris wheel was so amazing.

Still a Thrill

5   George Ferris's wheel was a hit with fair-goers. They rode for the thrill of rising 264 feet in the air. They rode for the joy of having a bird's-eye view of the world below. In fact, they rode the Ferris wheel for the same reasons we do when we go to an amusement park or a town fair today.

Timeline of American Amusement Rides

1799	1884	1893
The merry-go-round amuses in Salem, Massachusetts.	Coney Island in New York City gets the first American roller coaster.	The Ferris wheel first appears at the World's Fair in Chicago.

Making Electricity from Fruit

Electricity may have astonished the people of
Mr. Ferris's day, but you can make electricity with
common, everyday items.

Materials:

one lemon or orange

one 2-inch copper nail

one 2-inch zinc nail

one holiday light bulb with 2-inch leads (wires)

Procedure:

1. Roll the fruit around or gently squeeze to soften it.
    This gets the juices flowing inside the skin of the fruit.

2. Have a teacher or parent help you with this part of
    the experiment. Push the nails into the fruit, about
    2 inches apart. Do not let them touch each other.

3. With the help of an adult, remove one inch of
    insulation from the leads of the light bulb. Wrap one
    lead around the zinc nail, and wrap the other around
    the copper nail. You can use electrical tape or clips
    so that the wire stays on the nails.

4. Watch the light turn on.

1 Why is it important that paragraph 2 comes before paragraph 3?

   A To show why the fairgrounds were lit with many lights at night

   B To show why the city of Chicago was selected as the site of the World's Fair

   C To show why the Ferris wheel was invented and how it got its name

   D To show how the Exposition taught Americans about other cultures

   TEKS 5.11C

Tip

Think about how the information in paragraph 2 is connected to the information in paragraph 3.

---

2 What is the main idea of the article?

   F The Ferris wheel has changed a great deal since its creation.

   G The first Ferris wheel still stands at the Columbian Exposition.

   H The first Ferris wheel stood 264 feet high and held 2,000 people.

   J The Ferris wheel was created as a ride for the 1893 World's Fair.

   TEKS 5.11A

3 Which subheading would you look under to find information about the design of the Ferris wheel?

   A **A Wonderful Invention**

   B **The 1893 World's Fair**

   C **Ferris's Wheel**

   D **Still a Thrill**

   TEKS 5.11D

4 In what way was the Ferris wheel a fitting symbol of the World's Fair?

   F It was designed by an American inventor.

   G It was an extremely large structure.

   H It provided some amusement for children.

   J It created great excitement among the visitors.

   TEKS 5.11E

Tip

Think about all the ways the Ferris wheel and the World's Fair affected people.

24

Grade 5: Expository Text

5 Which of the following is a fact you could check by using an electronic encyclopedia?

A Ferris wheels are now so common that people do not consider why the ride was invented.

B Many people of the late nineteenth century were terribly frightened of electricity.

C The first Ferris wheel had cars that were much larger than the ones we ride in today.

D More people enjoyed the thrill of the ride than the bird's-eye view of the fairgrounds.

TEKS 5.11B

6 Look back at the timeline. In which year did the first roller coaster appear in the United States?

F 1799

G 1884

H 1890

J 1893

TEKS 5.13B

7 Look at the sequence chart below. One box is not in the correct order.

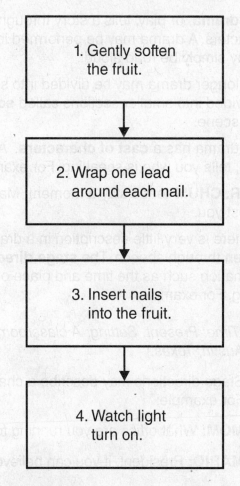

What is the correct order of steps for this procedure?

A 1, 3, 2, 4

B 3, 2, 1, 4

C 1, 4, 2, 3

D 4, 3, 2, 1

TEKS 5.13A

Name _____ Date _____

TEKS 5.2E, 5.5, 5.6A, 5.6B

Drama

Genre Overview

A **drama**, or play, tells a story through the words and actions of characters. A drama may be performed in a theater or on a school stage, or may simply be read aloud.

A longer drama may be divided into sections called **acts**. Acts may then be divided into smaller sections called **scenes**. The setting may change in each scene.

A drama has a **cast of characters**. A character's name, followed by a colon, tells you who is speaking. For example:

MR. CHU: Please stay a moment, Mario. I have an idea that I hope will interest you.

There is very little description in a drama. Almost all of the information is given through speech. The **stage directions** in a drama provide information such as the time and place of the story or a description of the setting. For example:

(*Time: Present. Setting: A classroom in an elementary school in Austin, Texas.*)

Stage directions may describe a character's feelings and actions. For example:

MOM: What office are you running for?

MARIO: President, if you can believe that. (*He laughs and shrugs.*)

Stage directions are given from the point of view of an actor on the stage. For example, *stage right* means to the actor's right, which is to the audience's left.

When planning a drama, as in planning any story, the author must decide how one event will follow another. This order, or **sequence**, of events leads the reader or audience through the action of a play to its conclusion.

If you are reading a play and come across a word you do not know, look up the word in a **dictionary**, **thesaurus**, or **glossary**.

Drama

| Read this selection. Then answer the questions that follow it. Fill in the circle of the correct answer on your answer document. |

A Force for Change

Cast of Characters: MARIO, MR. CHU, MOM, SUE, STUDENTS

ACT 1
Scene 1 (*Setting: A nearly empty classroom. The clock reads 2:55. MARIO, a fifth-grade student with a lively expression, slings his backpack over one shoulder. MR. CHU rises from his desk.*)

1   **MR. CHU:** Please stay a moment, Mario. I have an idea that I hope will interest you.

2   **MARIO:** Sure, Mr. Chu. Is this about my English report?

3   **Mr. CHU:** No, there is something else on my mind. Have you been paying any attention to the race for Student Council?

4   **MARIO:** No, that's not my thing. You know me—I love to shoot hoops. I leave <u>politics</u> to kids like Sue Gregory and Marshall Brown. (*Laughs*) I bet they could run the student government all by themselves!

5   **MR. CHU:** Should the same students always be our council leaders? Is that healthy for any government?

> **Tip**
>
> Notice that the stage directions are set in italic type. The characters do not read them aloud.

Grade 5: Drama

Name _____ Date _____

6   **MARIO:** (*Slowly setting down his backpack on a nearby desk*) Are you saying that kids like me should run for office? Not just the popular students?

7   **MR. CHU:** That's exactly what I'm suggesting. You know, I see something in you, Mario. You don't always speak up in class, but when you do, you say something intelligent. And you have drive—just look at how you perform on the basketball court. If you put your mind to it, you could be a force for change.

8   **MARIO:** I'll think it over, Mr. Chu. But I really don't think I could win an election. (*Exits stage left*)

Scene 2 (*Setting: MARIO'S home. MOM is doing paperwork at her desk. MARIO stands in the doorway, looking uncertain.*)

9   **MOM:** Come on in. You look like you're worried about something.

10   **MARIO:** (*Entering MOM'S study*) Well, I need to write a speech. It's sort of—a campaign speech.

11   **MOM:** What office are you running for?

12   **MARIO:** President, if you can believe that. (*He laughs and shrugs.*)

13   **MOM:** (*Rising to give him a hug*) I sure can believe it. And we can work on some ideas tonight, if you like…

Scene 3 (*Setting: The school auditorium, two weeks later*)

14   **SUE:** (*Beaming at the crowd*) I'm sure we'll be happy working together again in Student Council. I may have been a good vice-president last year, but I'll be an even stronger president this term! (*Exits stage right as STUDENTS applaud politely*)

15   **MARIO:** (*Walking confidently across the stage and taking his place at the podium; he gazes directly at the audience*) Good morning. I know I'm not as familiar a face as Sue, who just gave such a great speech. On the other hand, that might be a good thing, you know?

(*MR. CHU leans forward in his seat, listening intently*)

Grade 5: Drama

16   **MARIO:** A government is only as strong as all of its members, and that includes the voters. On a basketball team, knowing when to pass the ball is just as important as making baskets. It's that way on Student Council, isn't it? Knowing when to get opinions from others, listening carefully—that's good leadership. I like working with a team, and I have a lot of energy and enthusiasm. We have a great school, but there's always room for improvement, isn't there?

(*MARIO goes downstage and hands a stack of cards to STUDENT in the front row.*)

17   **MARIO:** These cards are for your ideas. Tell me what you think we could work on this year. As president, the cards will be my guide. Thank you. (*Goes back to his seat*)

(*STUDENTS start to whisper excitedly to one another. Then there is a loud burst of applause.*)

18   **MR. CHU:** (*Speaking softly to himself*) I think we've just seen our force for change.

> **Tip**
>
> Think about why Mario compares Student Council to a basketball team.

> **Tip**
>
> Look for an event that resolves the problem introduced in the first scene of the play.

Grade 5: Drama

Name _____ Date _____

1 How can you tell that this passage is a drama?

A It is told through words and actions.

B It has a cast of characters.

C It has stage directions.

D All of the above

TEKS 5.5

2 Look at this glossary entry for the word politics from paragraph 4.

> **politics:** the science or study of government

Which sentence uses the word politics in the same way as it is defined in the glossary entry?

F I think that George does politics too much.

G The teacher gave politics to the student leader.

H Our school has a great deal of politics.

J My brother's favorite classes in college are about politics.

TEKS 5.2E

3 When Mr. Chu asks, "Is that healthy for any government?" he is thinking about—

A making school government involve a wider group of students

B looking for the healthiest students to run Student Council

C voting to replace Student Council with another type of government

D giving a basketball player the chance to teach sports to students

TEKS 5.5

Tip
Consider how writers can use dialogue to suggest, rather than directly state, an idea.

4 The author starts a new scene after paragraph 8 to show that—

F a different problem is introduced in the plot

G a candidate has already won the election

H the elections for Student Council have started

J the time and place of the action have changed

TEKS 5.5

5 Use this chart of stage directions to draw a conclusion from the play.

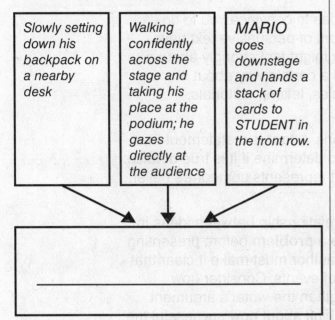

| *Slowly setting down his backpack on a nearby desk* | *Walking confidently across the stage and taking his place at the podium; he gazes directly at the audience* | *MARIO goes downstage and hands a stack of cards to STUDENT in the front row.* |

Which sentence belongs on the blank?

A Mario is just trying to please Mr. Chu by running for office.

B Mario wants to make friends with other student council leaders.

C Mario will not listen to other students if he is elected to office.

D Mario has grown sure of his ability to be a student leader.

TEKS 5.5

6 Mr. Chu is an important character because he—

F encourages Mario to think of himself as a leader

G teaches a fifth-grade class at an elementary school

H admires Mario's skills on the basketball court

J helps all the fifth-graders run for Student Council

TEKS 5.6B

Tip

Think about why Mario decides to run for Student Council president.

---

7 In Scene 3, what event resolves the problem?

A Students applaud after Sue's campaign speech.

B Mr. Chu listens closely to what Mario tells the other students.

C Mario sparks students' interest by handing out suggestion cards.

D Mario politely returns to his seat and leaves the podium free.

TEKS 5.6A

Grade 5: Drama

Name _____ Date _____

TEKS 5.2B, 5.10, 5.12A, 5.12B, RC-5(D), RC-5(E)

Persuasive Text

Overview

Persuasive text is a form of writing that tries to convince you to do something or to think a certain way. The authors of persuasive text have a strong **purpose**, or reason, for writing. They might feel strongly about a particular topic, or they might want you to feel a certain way about it. This type of writing includes text such as articles, letters, editorials, advertisements, and posters.

Persuasive text uses both facts and opinions. A **fact** is a statement that can be checked against an objective source to determine if it is true or false. An **opinion** *cannot* be proved true, because it represents someone's belief, or how that person feels about something.

As you read a persuasive text, notice the relationship between ideas in an argument. For instance, a writer must state a **problem** before presenting possible **solutions**. To convince readers, the author must make it clear that one event **causes** another event, or a series of events. Consider how **cause-and-effect** relationships work to strengthen the writer's argument. You should also **evaluate** a persuasive text. Think about how successful the writer is in making his or her argument.

To achieve a particular **purpose**, authors use many types of persuasive language in their writing. They might make you feel that it is your responsibility to do something, or make you feel guilty if you don't do it. They might **ask questions** to make you think a certain way about a topic. They might **stretch the truth—exaggerate—**about an idea to make a strong impression on you. They might even use misleading words to further their cause. As you read, think about how these devices support the **author's purpose**.

Since language is an important part of persuasive text, be sure to look for new vocabulary words as you read. Some of these words might have more than one **meaning**. As you read the sentence that contains the word, look for clues that tell you how the writer is using this word.

Persuasive Text

TEKS 5.2B, 5.10, 5.12A,
5.12B, RC-5(D), RC-5(E)

Persuasive Text

> **Read this selection. Then answer the questions that follow it.**
> **Fill in the circle of the correct answer on your answer document.**

Why Are Rain Forests Important?

1   Conservation, the protection of natural resources such as trees and water, is not new. However, during the past 25 years, scientists have become especially concerned about protecting the world's rain forests. Tropical rain forests are moist, green ecosystems. They are found in South America, Africa, and Australia. More than half of the plants and animals in the world live in rain forests.

2   Since European settlers arrived hundreds of years ago, people have harvested rain forest crops and products. These products include sugarcane, fruits, lumber, and rubber. The way people have harvested these products has harmed the soil. In addition, cutting down rain forest trees has put some kinds of plants and animals in danger of dying out.

> **Tip**
>
> The title asks a question about rain forests. It tells you that the article will answer the question or tell about the importance of rain forests.

Grade 5: Persuasive Text

3   Unfortunately, farmers in rain forests tend to grow the same <u>crops</u> on the same piece of land for two or three seasons in a row. Land needs time to rest between crops. Important minerals can be lost forever. Scientists know this, so they help people to use different ways of farming. They teach farmers to vary their crops and to give the soil time to rest so that it may be renewed.

4   How can cattle ranchers use their land more wisely? Amazon ranchers have tended to clear wooded land and to plant pastures where cattle can graze. This practice has caused the loss of many acres of rain forest. However, if ranchers plant trees on some of their land, they will lose no income while helping to save the forests. The new trees will provide shade for the animals. The acres that are planted will contain richer soil, so there are great advantages to this practice.

Tip

Think about what ranchers can do to cut down on the loss of rain forest land.

5   We do not know what will happen to our world if we continue to harm important ecosystems such as the rain forest. Will we all be doomed? Very soon, there may be no rain forests anyplace on Earth, and that would be a crime. We do know that one form of life depends on another. People should use this understanding to change the way they care for rain forests both today and in the future.

Persuasive Text

TEKS 5.2B, 5.10, 5.12A, 5.12B, RC-5(D), RC-5(E)

1 The author strongly supports the idea that—

A ranchers will want to plant trees on their land

B rain forests are not important to human beings

C human beings can affect the fate of the rain forests

D rain forests will shortly disappear from the Earth

TEKS 5.10

Tip
Think about the important point the author is making about protecting rain forest land.

2 In paragraph 3, the word <u>crops</u> means—

F plants grown by farmers for food

G cuts or bites the top off of

H bag-like part of a bird's food passage

J a short haircut

TEKS 5.2B

3 Look at the chart below.

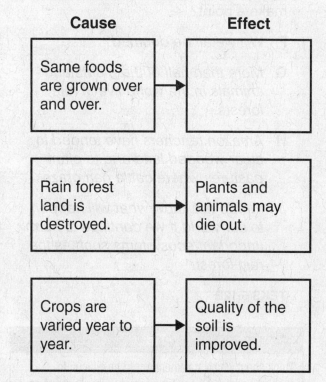

Cause	Effect
Same foods are grown over and over.	
Rain forest land is destroyed.	Plants and animals may die out.
Crops are varied year to year.	Quality of the soil is improved.

Which sentence belongs in the empty box?

A Farmers have better soil to use.

B Important minerals in soil are lost.

C Climate of the rain forests changes.

D World hunger is no longer a problem.

TEKS 5.12A

GO ON

Grade 5: Persuasive Text

4 Which statement stretches the truth to make a point?

F *Will we all be doomed?*

G *More than half of the plants and animals in the world live in rain forests.*

H *Amazon ranchers have tended to clear wooded land and to plant pastures where cattle can graze.*

J *We do not know what will happen to our world if we continue to harm important ecosystems such as the rain forest.*

TEKS 5.12B

> **Tip**
>
> Think about which statement would be difficult to support or defend. Look for a sentence that contains an exaggeration.

5 In paragraph 4, "lose no income" means—

A earn very little money

B lose all the money that they have

C earn the same amount of money

D use their money for other purposes

TEKS RC-5(E)

6 Why do acres planted with trees contain richer soil than acres that are used for cattle grazing?

F Ranchers only plant trees on fertile soil.

G Cattle choose the most fertile land to graze on.

H Plants and trees return minerals to the soil.

J Rich soil only exists where there is shade.

TEKS RC-5(D)

Grade 5: Persuasive Text

Name _____ Date _____

Poetry

Genre Overview

Poetry is a form of writing, often in rhyme, that tells a story or describes something. A poem **rhymes** when two or more lines end with the same sound. A poet may use a pattern of line lengths to create **rhythm** in a poem. Rhythm is the pattern of stressed and unstressed syllables in a line: BEAT the DRUM, and BLOW the HORN, for example. When we read a poem, it helps to know how to put the stress on the correct syllables.

A poet might use **figurative language** to describe something in a poem. Figurative language is language that goes beyond its literal meaning. Similes and metaphors are types of figurative language. **Similes** use the words *like* or *as* to compare two things. An example of a simile is *The guitar notes were like drops of honey*. This simile describes music with a sweet sound. **Metaphors** compare two things by saying that one thing *is* another thing. An example of a metaphor is *The girl who sang the solo was a nightingale*. This metaphor describes a girl who sings beautifully. Metaphors do not use the words *like* and *as* to compare.

Another way a poet might describe something is by using sensory language to appeal to one or more of the five senses. A poet might say, *The air clung to me like a soggy blanket* to show what a damp, uncomfortable day feels like. **Imagery** refers to pictures we form in our minds as we read. A poet might describe *high, silvery clouds* or an *old weathered barn* to give the readers a vivid picture of a scene. **Sound effects** also bring a poem to life. One type of sound effect is **alliteration**, in which two or more words in a line of poetry start with the same consonant letter—*tapping, twirling, twisting*, for instance. Sometimes, words that make us hear a poem are *onomatopoeic*, which means that the word imitates the actual sound: *creak, sizzle, pop!*

Poetry

TEKS 5.4, 5.8,
RC-5(D), RC-5(E)

**Read this selection. Then answer the questions that follow it.
Fill in the circle of the correct answer on your answer document.**

Ernie Gondry Did the Laundry

1   A nice young man named Ernie Gondry
     asked if he could do the laundry.
     "Just the whites," called his mother Jean,
     "Be sure you don't include a green!"

5   Ernie listened to Jean's advice,
     which is why he was so very nice.
     But one thing she should have said
     was, "Ernie, don't plop in a red."

     In the yawning mouth he placed a lump,
10 a red gumball of socks that made it jump.
     A-thump, a-thump, like a cannon shot,
     he pulled out the socks, but one he forgot.

     As Ernie waited for the washer to buzz,
     he started doing what a nice man does.
15 He picked up things and watched the clocks,
     not once fretting about the color of socks.

     He knew the washer would get out the dirt,
     and never thought the clothes would be hurt.
     When the washer growled its final sound,
20 He lifted the lid—this is what he found.

     That one red sock had done its trick,
     and Ernie started feeling sick.
     In his wildest dreams he'd never think,
     one red could turn those whites to pink.

GO ON ➡

Grade 5: Poetry

Name _____ Date _____

TEKS 5.4, 5.8,
RC-5(D), RC-5(E)

1 You can tell that "Ernie Gondry Did the Laundry" is a poem because it has—

A a lesson to teach the reader

B lines that end with words that rhyme

C a story to tell the reader

D characters and a narrator

TEKS 5.4

2 Which of these is an example of figurative language?

F *he was so very nice*

G *listened to Jean's advice*

H *like a cannon shot*

J *fretting about the color of socks*

TEKS 5.8

Tip
Remember that figurative language includes similes and metaphors.

3 In line 10, *red gumball of socks* means—

A two socks

B socks that have gum in them

C a clump of socks

D socks that can bounce

TEKS RC-5(D)

4 Look at the word web below.

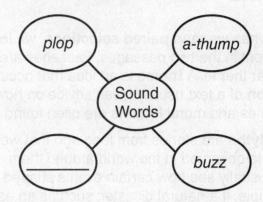

Which word goes in the blank?

F *do*

G *growled*

H *picked*

J *trick*

TEKS 5.4

5 Ernie's mother warned him about green clothes because she—

A knew they contained powerful dyes that stain material

B thought these articles of clothing were difficult to clean

C worried that Ernie would break the washing machine by overloading it

D hoped Ernie would forget about doing the laundry and go outside to play

TEKS RC-5(E)

Grade 5: Poetry

Name _____ Date _____

Paired Selections

Myths

When we read **paired selections**, we look for what is similar and different in the two passages. Passages are paired because they explore a similar theme. A **theme** is an idea that occurs throughout a text. The **moral lesson** of a text usually gives advice on how you can be a better person. Themes and moral lessons are often found in stories such as myths.

Myths are stories from long ago that were created to explain things that people observed in the world around them. If you look back in history, you can usually see how certain events shaped the myths of a culture. For example, if a natural disaster, such as an earthquake, affected a culture, you might be able to find mention of the earthquake in one of its myths.

Almost every culture has myths. Some of these stories are **origin myths** that tell how the world began. There are myths about how the sun and the moon came to light up the sky and about how oceans were formed. Many myths explain why we have four seasons and why we take in a harvest of food in the autumn. In fact, there is a myth for almost everything we see around us in nature.

You will find that myths contain all the elements of fiction. There are major and minor **characters**, a **conflict**, and a **solution**. As characters play their parts in a story, they reveal certain traits, or qualities. These qualities lead them to act in certain ways. A clever character will behave in an intelligent way, while a foolish character will make mistakes.

Like most stories, myths include **foreshadowing**, hints about what will happen later in the plot. For example, if we are told that a character is clever, we can expect that he or she will find a solution to a problem. When reading a myth, look for events and details that help you understand the characters, plot, and theme of the tale. Think about how you would **paraphrase**, or put the author's language into your own words. Finally, be prepared to **summarize** the main ideas and details.

Grade 5: Paired Selections

Paired Selections

> **Read the next two selections. Then answer the questions that follow them.**
> **Fill in the circle of the correct answer on your answer document.**

How Anansi Got His Stories

Adapted from Ashanti mythology

1   Long ago, there were no stories in the world. People gathered to eat and talk, but they had no tales to tell each other. This made them sad.

2   Anansi the clever spider thought he might be able to help. Anansi knew that all of the world's stories were being hoarded by Nyame way up in the sky. So one day Anansi asked Nyame, "How much would it cost to get those stories from you?"

3   "The cost would be very high," Nyame said playfully.

4   "Still, I would like to buy those stories from you," replied Anansi.

5   Nyame set a price that would be very hard to pay. If Anansi could capture the giant Python, the fierce Leopard, the stinging Hornets, and the magical Fairy, and bring them to Nyame, Anansi could have all the stories.

6   Anansi was small, but he always used his wits. He crawled into a palm tree where he knew the great Python was resting. Anansi said aloud, "My wife says that the great Python is longer than a palm branch, but I'm not sure I believe her."

7   Python heard this and explained with some pride that he was, truly, much longer than a palm branch. Anansi replied, "You're very long, but I don't believe you're that long."

8   The snake, not to be challenged, stretched himself along a palm branch to prove it, but it was very hard for him to lie down straight. "Perhaps if I tie your tail to the branch, we can see your great length," Anansi offered.

> **Tip**
>
> Think about how this event might foreshadow future events in the story.

9   The snake agreed, and Anansi tied him down. That was how Anansi caught the Python.

10   Anansi went into the forest and dug a large hole. Soon, Leopard strolled by and fell into the pit. Anansi was there to help him. "My dear friend, Leopard, let me help you out of this hole by spinning a rope of webs," he said. Anansi spun a web around the Leopard who was quickly captured.

11   To catch the stinging Hornets, Anansi filled a gourd with water. He poured it over the hornet's nest and cried out, "It's raining! Come stay dry in this empty gourd!" He sealed the gourd with the hornets buzzing inside.

12   Then Anansi made a pretty doll and covered her with sticky gum. He put the doll in front of a bowl of sweet yams. The Fairy happened by and took a bite of the yams, saying, "Thank you so much!" to the doll. Of course, the doll did not reply, so the Fairy shook it, getting herself stuck in the gum.

13   To Nyame's great surprise, Anansi returned with the Python, Leopard, Hornets, and Fairy. True to his promise, Nyame gave Anansi the spider these stories to tell for years to come.

Tip
Think about how Anansi's character traits lead to his success.

GO ON

Grade 5: Paired Selections

How Stories Came to the World

Adapted from Native American mythology

1   A long time ago, there were no stories in the world. Life was not easy for people, and it was especially hard in winter, when the wind whipped snow into tall peaks around the longhouses. The people huddled inside their homes but had no stories to amuse them over the long winter months.

2   One day, a clever boy set out into the snow to find food for his village. He was lucky and found food, which he immediately placed in his sack. The boy was tired, however, so before he began his journey back home, he set down his sack and leaned against a large stone, rubbing his feet. As he sat there, he noticed that the stone he rested upon was shaped almost like a man's head. Suddenly, he heard a deep voice ask, "Would you like to hear a story?"

> **Tip**
>
> Notice how the author describes the boy from the village.

3   The boy jumped up. "Who is there?" he yelled. He looked all around but saw no one.

4   "I am Great Stone," thundered the voice as the ground beneath the boy's feet started to rumble. "I will tell you a story."

5   "Go ahead and tell it," said the boy, pretending to be unafraid.

6   "First, I will need a little present. That food you have gathered will do," said the Great Stone.

7   The boy, being curious, placed his sack of food on the stone. The Great Stone then told a wonderful story of how the world was created. As the boy listened, a feeling of warmth came over him. He was no longer tired, and his feet no longer ached.

8   "I thank you, Great Stone," said the boy when the story was finished. "I will go home and share this story with the people. It will surely keep them warm on cold nights."

GO ON

Grade 5: Paired Selections

© Houghton Mifflin Harcourt Publishing Company

Paired Selections

TEKS 5.3A, 5.3B, 5.3C, 5.6A,
5.6B, RC-5(D), RC-5(E), RC-5(F)

9   When the boy returned home, the people were concerned that he had not brought any food. "Don't worry. Something wonderful has happened," he told them.

10   Everyone gathered around the fire and the boy told the story of how the world was created. The people grew warm and happy, and suddenly the winter night did not seem so dark and cold.

> **Tip**
>
> Think about how the conflict in this story is resolved.

11   All through the winter, the boy returned to the Great Stone, always bringing a gift. In return, the stone told amazing stories of wonder and adventure. The boy shared these stories with the people, and they repeated the tales to their children.

12   That is how stories came to the world. To this day, people tell stories to drive away the cold on long, winter nights. When a story is finished, everyone gives thanks to the storyteller, just as the boy gave gifts to the Great Stone long ago.

GO ON

Grade 5: Paired Selections

Name _____ Date _____

Use "How Anansi Got His Stories" to answer questions 1 and 2.

1 Anansi's main problem is that he—

A wants to become friends with Nyame, but the snake is dangerous

B struggles to win the trust and respect of the people in his village

C must find a way to get the world's stories from Nyame

D has to figure out a clever way to trap the stinging hornets in the gourd

TEKS 5.6B

Tip
Think about what Anansi sets out to do.

2 This myth explains how the—

F Ashanti people began to worship spiders

G powerful snake gained control of an Ashanti village

H Ashanti people came to believe in fairies

J custom of storytelling developed among the Ashanti

TEKS 5.3B

Use "How Stories Came to the World" to answer questions 3 and 4.

3 Which earlier event hints at how the people will respond to the boy's first story?

A The boy agrees to trade the sack of food for a story.

B The people gather around to hear the boy retell the Great Stone's story.

C The boy thanks the Great Stone for telling him the story.

D The boy forgets his cold and hunger while listening to the Great Stone.

TEKS 5.6A

4 This Native American myth most likely comes from a time when—

F a magical stone spoke to a child

G food was scarce for the tribe

H people did not know any stories

J snow fell for the first time

TEKS 5.3C

45

© Houghton Mifflin Harcourt Publishing Company

Use "How Anansi Got His Stories" and "How Stories Came to the World" to answer questions 5 through 8.

---

5 Look at the chart below.

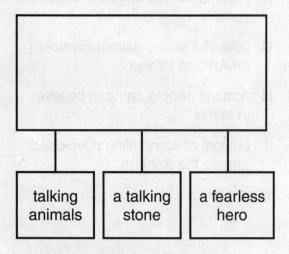

| talking animals | a talking stone | a fearless hero |

Which sentence belongs in the box?

A Myths were told only to children.

B Myths contain many obvious lies.

C Myths explain what the world used to be like.

D Myths contain unusual characters.

TEKS RC-5(D)

6 Which of the following best summarizes these two selections?

F In these myths, characters trick each other to get what they want. There is a lot of magic in each story, and they are both very entertaining.

G People in these myths are very sad until someone tells them a good story. All people enjoy stories if they are entertaining and have interesting characters.

H These myths each include a character who brings the art of storytelling to his or her people. The community finds wisdom and entertainment in the stories.

J Characters in a myth are not real people. Animals and stones are more important than people because the stories are about magic, not about real life.

TEKS RC-5(E)

GO ON

Name _____ Date _____

TEKS 5.3A, 5.3B, 5.3C, 5.6A, 5.6B, RC-5(D), RC-5(E), RC-5(F)

7 Which theme is found in both selections?

A Animals can be as clever as people.

B Stories are an important part of a culture.

C A young person can be as wise as an older person.

D It is best to use your mind, and not force, to solve problems.

TEKS 5.3A

Tip
After you read each answer choice, ask yourself if it applies to both of the selections.

8 A difference between the two selections is that the Anansi story—

F tells how a custom began

G is set in the distant past

H has a third-person narrator

J involves playing a trick

RC-5(F)

STOP

47

> **Read this selection. Then answer the questions that follow it.
> Fill in the circle of the correct answer on your answer document.**

Bonesy and Isabel

by Michael J. Rosen

1   Before Isabel came to the house on Sunbury Road, thirty-five other creatures were living there. At least thirty-five—and that's not counting all the creatures that couldn't be counted. Three horses grazed the grassy fields. Eleven ducks paddled a pond that had been dug and filled only a few years ago. Eight or nine cats prowled the place— some inside and some outside. And nine dogs called that house their home: outside dogs that used to be strays (mixed-up breeds and many sizes), except for one inside dog, a twelve-year-old Labrador retriever named Bonsey.

2   And there were two people who cared for all these countable creatures. They were the ones who had brought Isabel from El Salvador.

3   The main house on Sunbury Road had once been a cabin, but over the years, the many owners had made one addition after another. Now there are fifteen rooms, as well as a pair of barns, gardens in all the sunny and partly sunny spots, a tool shed, an empty corncrib, timber and picket fences, part of a pine forest, a deck, and a pasture, too. The whole place rambles like a long story. And each creature who lives in or around or above the house on Sunbury Road knows a different part of that story.

4   The barn swallows and nighthawks could tell you about the chimney smoke and the antenna's perches, where the roof slates have cracked and the gutters have clogged with leaves.

5   The horse knows the barnyard's circles, the mole and rabbit holes in the fields, the scrambling gravel along the roads, and how far it is from here to most anywhere.

6   The cats spy on everyone, nosing into nooks and niches where crickets *chirr* and mice skedattle. Still, whatever stories the cats discover they don't tell a living soul.

Reading
PRACTICE

TEKS 5.2B, 5.6A, 5.6B, 5.6C,
5.8, RC-5(D)

7   But the nine dogs in Isabel's new house share a single story. It's the story of the people who took them from the dangerous roads where each had been abandoned. Of course, they all know the faint wind's gossip of scents and the story of the fences where they bark to passersby: *Don't bother our house.* Yet the real story they like to tell is about the people of the house who speak to them in a strange language—words that, most of the time, just mean, *We care for you.*

8   When Isabel came to the house, she knew only a few words of that strange language, English—about as much as the dogs knew, which was a lot more than the horses would ever know, and a little more than the cats admitted knowing. As for the uncountable birds, Isabel quickly learned the nighthawks' *peent, peent,* and the swallows' rapid *tat-tat-tat-tat.*

9   And so Isabel spent her summer listening to the animals who showed her all they knew about the place. Though she didn't understand their busy language, it sounded good to her. The animals of Sunbury Road spoke like the wandering mules and chickens and goats from the roads of El Salvador Isabel remembered.

10   Isabel called the people who lived in the house "Vera" and "Ivan." They were the ones who groomed the horses, flea-dipped the cats, untangled burrs from the dogs' coats, and stuffed the bird feeders with suet. They were the ones who had brought Isabel from a country farther away than any of the resident birds could report from their high-up views.

11   People were always visiting Isabel's new house—especially at dinnertime when there would be clinking glasses and clouds of laughter. Although Isabel couldn't often understand what was funny, she at least understood that Vera and Ivan and their friends were happy. Laughing in English sounded just like laughing in Spanish.

12   It was Bonesy, the one inside dog, who became Isabel's closest companion. Isabel even recognized the word "companion" the first time Vera pronounced it slowly; it sounded so much like *compañero.* Bonesy was allowed inside the house because he was old. And because he had lost most of his teeth, he was allowed to eat table scraps. And because he had arthritis, Bonesy was even allowed to stay under the dining room table, where scraps could be slipped to him under the tablecloth. He never begged. He just waited—or slept. While Vera and Ivan and their guests would laugh, Isabel would feed Bonesy the soft leftovers from her plate. She would slip off her shoes and stroke Bonesy's coat with her bare toes.

Grade 5: Reading Practice

13   And so it was always-awaiting Bonesy who helped Isabel study English. A little of it, anyway. Under the dining room table with the sleepy dog, Isabel would sound out the English words in her new books. Though Bonesy didn't know if it was right when Isabel said *hor-SES* or when she said *HOR-ses,* he rewarded her with licks for practicing beside him. The warm breeze from Bonesy's nose would <u>riffle</u> the pages of her book. And whenever Isabel said *Bonesy* or *Good dog*! or *¡Perro bueno!*, the old retriever would thump his tail against the rug. Whatever language Isabel spoke, Bonesy seemed to know she was saying what his other humans often said: *I care for you.*

Name _____ Date _____

1 In paragraph 3, "rambles like a long story" means that the property on Sunbury Road is—

A not a real place, but belongs only to this story

B a good subject for a story about country life

C made up of many parts that go on and on

D a noisy place, with all the barking dogs and other creatures

TEKS 5.8

2 Read this sentence from paragraph 10 of the selection.

> *They were the ones who groomed the horses, flea-dipped the cats, untangled burrs from the dogs' coats, and stuffed the bird feeders with suet.*

This sentence shows that Vera and Ivan are—

F caring

G tired

H bothered

J struggling

TEKS RC-5(D)

3 How can you tell this selection is written in third-person omniscient point of view?

A A narrator is also a character.

B The narrator knows what many characters observe and know.

C Bonesy is telling the story.

D The narrator knows what one character observes and knows.

TEKS 5.6C

4 Which words from the selection appeal to your sense of hearing?

F *wandering mules*

G *crickets chirr*

H *story of the fences*

J *soft leftovers*

TEKS 5.8

5 After Isabel spends a summer listening to the animals, she—

A starts to miss the roads of El Salvador

B starts to feel more at home in a new place

C stops spending time indoors with Bonesy

D stops trying to learn how to speak English

TEKS 5.6A

GO ON

Grade 5: Reading Practice

Reading
PRACTICE

TEKS 5.2B, 5.6A, 5.6B, 5.6C,
5.8, RC-5(D)

6 Why does Isabel feel comfortable with Bonesy?

F Bonesy is a quiet, peaceful companion for Isabel.

G Bonesy is just like a dog Isabel had in El Salvador.

H Bonesy eats Isabel's table scraps at meal times.

J Bonesy is the only dog that sleeps inside the house.

TEKS 5.6B

7 What is Isabel's problem in the selection?

A She struggles to overcome a fear of the dogs of Sunbury Road.

B She feels very homesick for her family and friends in El Salvador.

C She does not feel comfortable with the couple who have adopted her.

D She struggles to understand the language spoken by her new family.

TEKS 5.6B

8 Which word from paragraph 13 helps the reader understand what <u>riffle</u> means?

F *rewarded*

G *breeze*

H *nose*

J *thump*

TEKS 5.2B

9 Look at the details in this inference map.

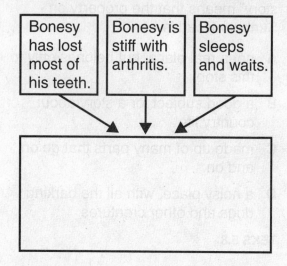

Which inference belongs in the blank box?

A Bonesy helps Isabel study English.

B Vera and Ivan enjoy caring for Bonesy.

C Isabel feeds Bonesy table scraps.

D Bonesy needs extra care and protection.

TEKS RC-5(D)

10 Vera and Ivan are important to the selection because they—

F take care of many animals

G give Bonesy and Isabel a home

H teach Isabel English words

J have many friends come to dinner

TEKS 5.6B

Grade 5: Reading Practice

> **Read this selection. Then answer the questions that follow it.**
> **Fill in the circle of the correct answer on your answer document.**

from Out of Darkness: The Story of Louis Braille

by Russell Freedman

1 Visions of dots and more dots danced in Louis's head. He wanted to simplify Captain Barbier's system so that each dotted symbol could be "read" with a quick touch of the finger.

2 His days were filled with classes and school activities, so he experimented whenever he could find the time—between classes, on weekends, at night in the <u>dormitory</u>. When everyone else had gone to bed, and the only sound was the breathing of his sleeping classmates, he would take out his stylus and paper and begin to juggle dots. Often, he would doze off himself, the stylus grasped in his hand as though he wanted to keep on working in his sleep.

3 On some nights, he lost all track of time. He would be sitting on the edge of his bed, punching dots, when the rumbling of the wagons on the cobblestones outside told him that morning had come.

4 After staying up all night, he fell asleep in class. And like several other students, he developed a hacking cough. Winter coughs were common at the Institute. The old school building always felt damp and cold.

5 Louis's mother worried about him when he came home for vacation. He looked so pale and gaunt. She wanted to fatten him up, and she insisted that he go to bed early. Monique would climb the stairs to the garret bedroom, tuck Louis in, and kiss him good-night, as though he were still a little boy.

6 A few weeks of fresh country air did wonders. Louis's cough vanished. He felt revived. On fine mornings, he would walk down the road with his cane, carrying a stylus, writing board, and paper in his knapsack. He would sit on a grassy slope, basking in the sun and working patiently as he punched dots into paper. People would pass by and call out, "Hello there, Louis! Still making pinpricks?" They weren't sure what he was trying to do, but whatever it was, he was obviously lost in thought.

Grade 5: Reading Practice

7   Gradually, Louis managed to simplify Captain Barbier's system, but
he wasn't satisfied. The dotted symbols he came up with were never
simple enough. Sometimes he shouted in frustration and ripped the
paper he was working on to shreds.

8   Then an idea came to him—an idea for an entirely different
approach. It seemed so obvious! Why hadn't he thought of it before?

9   Captain Barbier's symbols were based on *sounds*—that was the
problem! There were so many sounds in the French language. With
sonography, a dozen dots or more might be needed to represent one
syllable, as many as a hundred dots for a single word.

10   Instead of sounds, suppose the dot-and-dash symbols represented
letters of the alphabet? The alphabet would be so much easier to
work with.

11   Of course, Louis could not simply have one dot stand for *a*, two
dots for *b*, and so on. That way, a blind reader would have to count
twenty-six dots to read the letter *z*. Additional dots would be needed
for numbers and punctuation marks.

12   But now that he had changed his thinking, Louis made real
progress. He invented a simple code that allowed him to represent
any letter of the alphabet within the space of a fingertip. At the
beginning of the fall term in 1824, he was ready to demonstrate his
new system. He had been working on it for three years.

13   First, he asked for a meeting with the school's director, Dr. Pignier.
Louis sat in a big armchair opposite Pignier's desk, a writing board
and paper on his lap, a stylus in his hand. He asked the director to
select a passage from a book, any book he chose. "Read from it
slowly and distinctly," Louis said, "as if you were reading to a sighted
friend who was going to write down all your words."

14   Pignier picked a book from the shelf behind him. He opened it and
began to read. Louis bent over his writing board and paper, his hand
flying as he punched dots. After a few lines, he told Pignier, "You can
read faster."

15   When Pignier finished reading the passage, Louis ran his finger
over the raised dots on the back of the paper, as if to reassure himself.
Then, without hesitating, he read every word he had taken down, at
about the same speed as the director had read them.

GO ON

Grade 5: Reading Practice

16   Pignier couldn't believe his ears. He picked out another book, another passage, and asked Louis to repeat the demonstration. Then, rising from the desk with a burst of emotion, the director embraced Louis and praised him.

17   Soon the entire school was talking about Louis's new language of raised dots. Dr. Pignier called an assembly to introduce the students and teachers to the new system. Louis sat in the middle of a big classroom, working with his stylus as one of the sighted teachers read a poem aloud. The other sighted teachers leaned forward in their seats, watching Louis's hand move across the paper. The blind instructors and students cocked their heads and listened as the point of the stylus punched out dots.

18   Then Louis stood up. He cleared his throat and recited the poem, his fingers moving as he spoke, without missing a word or making an error. When he finished, an excited murmur filled the room and everyone crowded around him.

19   Louis was just fifteen years old when he demonstrated the first workable form of his system. During the next few years, he would continue to improve and add to his system, but he had already devised the basic alphabet that would open the doors of learning to blind people all over the world.

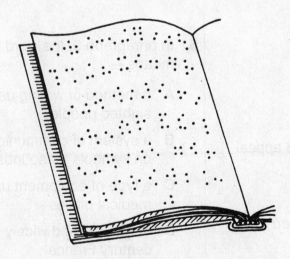

Grade 5: Reading Practice

GO ON

1 What literary language does the author use to show how hard Louis is thinking about a solution?

A *Visions of dots and more dots danced in Louis's head.*

B *He wanted to simplify Captain Barbier's system.*

C *The only sound was the breathing of his sleeping classmates*

D *After staying up all night, he fell asleep in class.*

TEKS 5.7

2 Which words from the selection best help the reader understand what <u>dormitory</u> means in paragraph 2?

F *sleeping classmates*

G *juggle dots*

H *school activities*

J *between classes*

TEKS 5.2B

3 Which words from paragraph 3 appeal to the sense of hearing?

A *lost all track of time*

B *sitting on the edge of his bed*

C *punching dots*

D *rumbling of the wagons on the cobblestones*

TEKS 5.7

4 Read this sentence from paragraph 6 of the selection.

> *He would sit on a grassy slope, basking in the sun and working patiently as he punched dots into paper.*

What do the sensory details in this sentence show a reader?

F They show that Louis was too tired to play games.

G They show that Louis did not enjoy his vacation.

H They show that Louis enjoyed working alone outside.

J They show that the countryside around Louis's home was hilly.

TEKS 5.8

5 In paragraph 9, the word <u>sonography</u> means—

A a method of writing used only by sighted people

B a system of communication based on symbols for sounds

C a type of equipment used in medical offices

D a system used widely in nineteenth-century France

TEKS 5.2A

6 Which of the following is the best summary of this selection?

F Despite health problems, Louis Braille attended a school for the blind that was often damp and cold. He worked very hard to invent a new system of reading and writing for the blind. Soon other people used the Braille system.

G Louis Braille invented a new system of reading and writing for the blind. Louis's system was based on the alphabet rather than on sounds. The Braille system eventually improved the lives of blind people.

H Louis Braille invented a system of reading and writing that is still used by blind people. Louis sat in a big armchair and demonstrated the new method to the director of the school he attended. The director hugged and praised Louis and told the teachers and students to try the Braille system.

J The inventor of the Braille system was Louis Braille, a blind boy who lived in France. He thought only of how to make his new system better than that of Captain Barbier. Louis worked very hard, even during vacations. Finally, he succeeded with his new method of reading and writing. His symbols were based on the alphabet.

TEKS RC-5(E)

7 Look at the following chart.

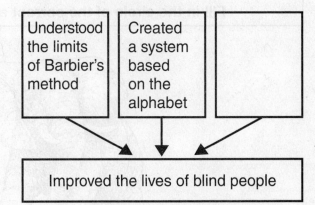

Understood the limits of Barbier's method	Created a system based on the alphabet	

Improved the lives of blind people

Which information belongs in the empty space?

A Was often ill as a child

B Convinced others to try his system

C Attended a school for the blind in France

D Was frustrated when he ran into problems

TEKS 5.7

8 This selection is of interest mainly because it—

F tells about a boy who was respected by teachers and other students

G records a major advance in the education of people with physical challenges

H describes the lives of French people in the middle of the nineteenth century

J explains why the schools of long ago were less healthful places than the schools of today

TEKS 5.3C

STOP

57

Name _____ Date _____

Reading
PRACTICE

TEKS 5.2B, 5.2E, 5.10, 5.11A,
5.11B, 5.11C, 5.11E,
5.14C, RC-5(D)

> **Read this selection. Then answer the questions that follow it.**
> **Fill in the circle of the correct answer on your answer document.**

Something in the Elephants' Silence

by April Pulley Sayre

1   For fifteen years Katy Payne and her husband, Roger Payne,
studied whale song in the Pacific and northern Atlantic Oceans.
(Whale scientist Christopher Clark was one of Roger's students.)
The Paynes' base camp for studying humpback whales was a remote
beach in Argentina where they lived and raised their children. When
the Payne children grew up, Roger continued studying whales. But
Katy decided she wanted a new project all her own.

2   Katy Payne knew that elephants, like whales, live in family groups
and have complex behaviors, so she thought she might like to study
them. In 1984, to get a feel for elephants and their lives, she arranged
to spend a week with the elephants at the Washington Park Zoo in
Portland, Oregon. During that week, she sat outside the elephants' pen.
She watched and listened to them. She heard the elephants rumble,
trumpet, bellow, snuffle, and growl as they interacted with one another.

3   On the plane home from Oregon to New York, the vibration of the
airplane reminded her of the way the air had sometimes felt near the
elephants. She'd felt the same thing as a child, listening to a pipe
organ in a church. The organist had played lower and lower notes,
until her ears could not hear the notes clearly, but her body could feel
the shuddering <u>vibrations</u>. *Perhaps the elephants were making hidden
sounds, too,* she thought. *Maybe they were making infrasound.*

Grade 5: Reading Practice

Name _____ Date _____

4   Infrasound is any sound with a frequency below twenty hertz. That is below the range of sound that people's ears can hear. Lower-frequency sounds, such as infrasound, can be received easily only by a big surface. The human eardrum is too small. Yet the human diaphragm, the muscular membrane just below the ribs, shakes in response to infrasound. Scientist Bill Barklow likens the feeling of infrasound to standing at a parade when the bass drum comes by and makes your body shake.

5   Scientists know that fin whales and blue whales make infrasound. But no one before Katy Payne had realized that land animals might be able to make infrasound, too. People had always wondered how male and female elephants found each other across the great distances of the African savanna. And sometimes elephant herds seemed to react to one another's activities—even when those activities were happening miles away.

6   The idea that elephants were "talking" without people hearing them was exciting. But Payne wasn't sure she was right. She needed proof. So she borrowed special equipment that could measure infrasound, and, with biologist Bill Langbauer and friend Elizabeth Marshall Thomas, Payne returned to the zoo to study the elephant sounds. They spent a month recording sounds in the elephant enclosures and taking notes on the elephants' behavior.

7   The tape recorders they used recorded sounds at very slow speeds. Later on, the scientists could play the tapes at regular speed or high speed to raise the pitch of the calls. (The same thing happens when a recording of a person's voice is played at a high speed—it sounds higher and squeakier, like a chipmunk chirping.) Raising the pitch of the infrasonic elephant calls makes an even bigger difference. At normal speeds, the calls are so low in pitch that people can't hear them. But at high speeds, the sounds can be heard clearly.

8   When the team returned home from a month of recording elephant sounds, they still weren't sure that they'd found infrasound. Back at the lab in Ithaca, Payne and biologist Carl Hopkins hooked up the recordings to a spectrograph, which translated the sounds into dots and dashes, creating spectrograms just like the sound pictures Christopher Clark studies for whale research. Payne played part of a seemingly silent recording that had been made when she had felt vibrations in the air. The machine showed the recording was full of calls! Played at high speed, the infrasonic calls sounded like cows mooing. It was the first time anyone had heard elephants communicating in this way. Payne had found something extraordinary.

Grade 5: Reading Practice

Name _____ **Date** _____

Reading
PRACTICE

TEKS 5.2B, 5.2E, 5.10, 5.11A,
5.11B, 5.11C, 5.11E,
5.14C, RC-5(D)

Cracking the Code

9   During the sixteen years since the discovery of elephant infrasound, Payne has continued studying elephants calling, both in zoos and in the wild. She formed the Elephant Listening Project at Cornell University's Lab of Ornithology's Bioacoustics Research Program. As part of her research Payne had spent years analyzing tapes and video recordings to figure out which elephants are giving which calls. Linking calls to callers is difficult. Elephants don't necessarily open their mouths or flap their ears when they are calling. And they don't always move when they hear something.

10   Payne also watches the videos to see what the elephants were doing when they were calling. She and other scientists hope to create an "elephant dictionary" of what each call means. Figuring this out is challenging. Infrasonic elephant calls can travel for miles. A scientist may watch elephants close by, looking for reactions to the calls, but the most interesting reaction may be from an elephant miles away, out of the scientist's view. "It's a trick and a half to figure out what this communication is all about," says Payne.

11   Nevertheless, scientists have begun to decode some of the calls. Trumpeting, the loud sound elephants make, is used in times of excitement, when elephants are playing, fighting, or alarmed by a predator such as a lion. A special humming call is made by mother elephants when they are near their newborns. Female elephants, when trying to attract a male, make a low-pitched call that can last for up to forty-five minutes.

12   "We are beginning to understand what they are saying to each other...we can draw some conclusions. This is terribly exciting," says Payne.

Invitation for a Scientific Conference on Elephant Research

Time and Place: January 25, 2013, at The Elephant Park

The conference directors are currently accepting research papers on a wide variety of topics.

Areas of interest include: wildlife management; threatened elephant populations; elephant communication; emergency care for wounded elephants

If you are working on elephant research and would like to join in the conference, please contact us at:

www.elephanttalk/news

Grade 5: Reading Practice

Name _____ Date _____

Reading
PRACTICE

TEKS 5.2B, 5.2E, 5.10, 5.11A,
5.11B, 5.11C, 5.11E, 5.14C,
RC-5(D)

1 The author organizes paragraphs 1 through 3 by—

A describing how Katy Payne became interested in elephant communication

B comparing humpback whales in Argentina to elephants in the United States

C explaining why Katy Payne needed her own research project on animals

D listing the various kinds of unusual noises made by elephants in the zoo

TEKS 5.11C

2 The author probably wrote this selection to—

F share information about an interesting scientific discovery

G entertain the reader with some fun facts about wild animals

H convince students to study animal communication in depth

J teach readers the importance of finding meaningful work

TEKS 5.10

3 In paragraph 3, which word helps the reader understand what <u>vibrations</u> means?

A *air*

B *shuddering*

C *hidden*

D *sounds*

TEKS 5.2B

4 Look at the chart below. Which detail belongs in the blank box?

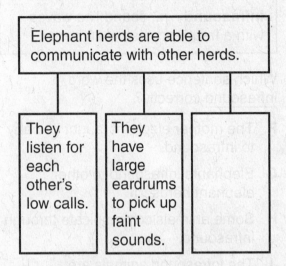

F Elephants make infrasonic sounds.

G Elephants are sometimes kept in zoos.

H Elephants live in family groups.

J Elephants are found mostly in Africa.

TEKS RC-5(D)

5 What resource would you use to check the facts in paragraph 8?

A The latest articles on elephant infrasound

B A biographical article about Christopher Clark

C A recent book about whales and dolphins

D A website for people who want to protect elephants

TEKS 5.11B

GO ON

Grade 5: Reading Practice

Name _____ Date _____

6 Look at the glossary entry below.

> **infrasound** *n.,* sound-like waves with a frequency below 20 hertz

Which sentence uses the word <u>infrasound</u> correctly?

F The mother elephant taught its baby to infrasound.

G Elephants infrasound to other elephant herds.

H Some animals communicate through infrasound.

J The infrasound animals are interesting to study.

TEKS 5.2E

7 How does the inclusion of the examples of the low notes of pipe organs and the movement of an airplane help the reader better understand this article?

A Each has been the subject of study by the scientist Katy Payne.

B Each can only be detected when recorded at an extremely slow speed.

C Each uses a range of sound that can only be heard when played back on a tape recorder.

D Each produces vibrations that can be felt rather than heard clearly by human ears.

TEKS 5.11E

8 What important information appears in the section **Cracking the Code**?

F How spectrographs work

G How cows and elephant noises are alike

H How Christopher Clark studied whale sounds

J How Payne learned to interpret elephant sounds

TEKS 5.11A

9 The writer of the invitation to the scientific conference believes that—

A many people are studying the problems of elephants

B it is too late to solve the problems of elephants in the wild

C sharing information about elephants will help these animals

D we already have enough information about elephants

TEKS 5.14 C

Name _____ Date _____

**Read this play. Then answer the questions that follow it.
Fill in the circle of the correct answer on your answer document.**

A Life of Adventure

Cast of Characters: *DAD, SELENA, UNCLE FRANK, PAULINA, VOICE OF ASTRONAUT NEIL ARMSTRONG*

ACT I

Scene 1 (*Setting: Lights up on the playground of an elementary school in Houston. Paulina is playing hopscotch. Selena, Paulina's twin sister, enters stage right and climbs the jungle gym.*)

1   **SELENA:** (*Calling loudly across the playground*) Hey, Paulina! Come over here and climb to the space station with me!

2   **PAULINA:** (*Unwillingly leaving her game and crossing the playground to the jungle gym*) If you don't mind, I'd rather not climb all the way up there. It makes me dizzy to look down.

3   **SELENA:** That's ridiculous! Anyone would think you were really going into outer space. Come up right now!

4   **PAULINA:** Well, okay, but not all the way to the top. (*She starts climbing slowly, pausing to get her balance on the rungs of the jungle gym as the lights go down.*) I wish you liked hopscotch, though.

Grade 5: Reading Practice

Name _____ Date _____

Reading
PRACTICE

TEKS 5.2A, 5.2E, 5.3C, 5.5',
5.6A, 5.6B, 5.8, RC-5(D),
RC-5(E)

Scene 2 *(Setting: Lights up in a living room. Dad and Uncle Frank are seated in front of a small television.)*

5   **DAD:** We'll remember this date for the rest of our lives—10:00 P.M. on July 20, 1969. The date we saw people first walk on the moon.

(Paulina and Selena enter stage right.)

6   **SELENA:** *(Hands on her hips)* We could have been watching this at Uncle Frank's house tonight, Paulina, on a bigger TV. Except you never want to go anywhere, so he had to come over here!

7   **UNCLE FRANK:** *(To Selena)* It's no problem. I'm glad to be here. *(To Dad)* I can't believe this is happening! They actually landed on the moon.

8   **DAD:** Watch, kids. You're about to see history being made.

9   **PAULINA:** *(Tossing back her hair)* So what if I like staying at home, Selena?

10   **SELENA:** You never want to do anything different. Or eat anything different. *(Imitating her sister's voice)* "I only eat peanut butter for lunch and macaroni and cheese for dinner." I'm not like you. I like to have adventures. It's boring at home. *(Paulina sits on the couch; Selena sits on the floor, away from her sister.)*

11   **DAD:** I think if you stopped talking for a few minutes, Selena, you'd have an adventure right here in your own living room.

12   **UNCLE FRANK:** I thought twins were supposed to be friends.

13   **PAULINA:** We are friends. We're just different from each other.

14   **SELENA:** Paulina should try something different once in awhile.

15   **DAD:** Listen. One of the astronauts is talking. Neil Armstrong.

16   **VOICE OF NEIL ARMSTRONG** *(From television)* I'm at the foot of the ladder. The lunar module footpads are only depressed in the surface about 1 or 2 inches. It's almost like a powder. I'm going to step off the ladder now.

17   **SELENA:** *(Pointing excitedly)* Look, he's stepping around deep craters on the moon! What would that be like? Can you imagine?

18   **PAULINA:** I think it would be scary.

GO ON

Grade 5: Reading Practice

TEKS 5.2A, 5.2E, 5.3C, 5.5, 5.6A, 5.6B, 5.8, RC-5(D), RC-5(E)

19   **SELENA:** He's really far from home! Can you imagine just stepping into some kind of strange powdery stuff that no human being has ever seen?

20   **PAULINA:** You're right. That would be kind of amazing. And Armstrong is on the chilly side of the moon.

21   **SELENA:** Dad, what happens if their spaceship breaks down? Will anyone be able to come and help them?

22   **DAD:** I'm sure that we would think of some way to help them.

23   **UNCLE FRANK:** Look! He did it! He stepped off the ladder onto the moon!

24   **VOICE OF NEIL ARMSTRONG:** (*From television*) That's one small step for man, one giant leap for mankind.

25   **PAULINA:** (*Clapping her hands excitedly*) Think about this. He can look up and see Earth in the sky. Nobody has ever been able to do that before.

26   **VOICE OF NEIL ARMSTRONG:** (*From television*) It has a stark beauty all its own. It's like much of the high desert of the United States. It's different, but it's very pretty out here.

27   **PAULINA:** I do like the desert, Selena. Remember when we went to Big Bend National Park?

28   **SELENA:** (*Softly*) All of that open space made me feel so small. It made me feel a little scared.

(*Paulina sits next to Selena on the floor and puts her arm around her.*)

29   **PAULINA:** I thought it was pretty cool.

(*Selena and Paulina look at each other. Then they burst out laughing.*)

ACT II

Scene 1 (*Setting: Twelve years later. Lights up on Dad and Selena sitting together at a kitchen table.*)

30   **SELENA:** (*Glancing at the clock on the wall*) I wonder why she's so late. That's not like Paulina at all. She's always on time.

31   **DAD:** Maybe her flight was delayed. By the way, how is *your* work going?

Grade 5: Reading Practice

Name _____ Date _____

Reading
PRACTICE

TEKS 5.2A, 5.2E, 5.3C, 5.5,
5.6A, 5.6B, 5.8, RC-5(D),
RC-5(E)

32   **SELENA:** Well, it's fine. I like helping other people find
<u>employment</u>. And I enjoy talking with people about their goals. So I
guess I picked the right career.

33   **DAD:** That's fine, then. Well, should we start making dinner?
Maybe by the time it's on the table, Paulina will be here.

34   **SELENA:** Sure! I've wanted to try out a new chili recipe.

35   **DAD:** You've turned out to be a great cook. *(He smiles, as if
remembering something from the past. Lights go down as father and
daughter start making preparations for the meal.)*

Scene 2 *(The kitchen, two hours later)*

36   **PAULINA:** *(Setting down her fork with a contented sigh)* That was
delicious. I don't have much time to cook these days, you know.

37   **DAD:** Well, you're always flying back and forth across the country.

38   **SELENA:** Who would have thought that *you'd* be the one to end up
with the exciting job?

39   **PAULINA:** I do like being a pilot. No flight ever seems too long. And
when we land and I get to explore a new city, it's incredibly thrilling.
But I do love returning to Houston as often as possible.

40   **DAD:** My two girls. The one who stayed on the ground...and the
one who found out that she loved the sky.

(All three begin to laugh softly, thinking back. . .)

Grade 5: Reading Practice

Name _____ Date _____

Reading
PRACTICE

TEKS 5.2A, 5.2E, 5.3C, 5.5,
5.6A, 5.6B, 5.8, RC-5(D),
RC-5(E)

1 Which of these is not true of a drama?

   A It is told through words and actions.

   B It has a cast of characters.

   C It has stage directions.

   D It is told without dialogue.

   TEKS 5.5

2 Who are the two main characters in this drama?

   F Dad and Uncle Frank

   G Paulina and Selena

   H Selena and Dad

   J Neil Armstrong and Uncle Frank

   TEKS 5.6B

3 What event introduces the problem?

   A Selena insists that Paulina climb the jungle gym.

   B Selena does not want to sit on the sofa with Paulina.

   C Dad wants the girls to watch the moon landing.

   D Uncle Frank does not want the twins to argue so much.

   TEKS 5.6A

4 What can the reader infer about a drama?

   F A drama can only have one setting.

   G Dramas do not have plots composed of events.

   H The scenes in a drama are like the chapters in a book.

   J There are few if any characters in a drama.

   TEKS 5.5

5 Look at this entry from a glossary.

   lunar: _adj.,_ of or like the moon

   Which sentence shows the word <u>lunar</u> used correctly?

   A The lunar surface has many rocky areas.

   B The spaceship headed straight for the lunar.

   C I often gaze at the stars and the lunar.

   D Our class studied the lunar last month.

   TEKS 5.2E

6 Look at this web of sensory details from the play.

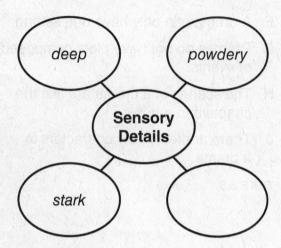

Which word completes the web of sensory details?

F *talking*

G *breaks*

H *chilly*

J *desert*

TEKS 5.8

7 When Neil Armstrong said, "That's one small step for man, one giant leap for mankind," he meant—

A he only took small steps on the moon's surface

B the spaceship leaped through outer space

C the moon landing represented great progress

D many people participated in the flight to the moon

TEKS RC-5(E)

8 Selena's reaction to the moon landing shows that she—

F wishes she could be an astronaut

G does not always feel adventurous

H thinks her sister is being foolish

J is not really interested in space missions

TEKS RC-5(D)

9 In paragraph 32, the word <u>employment</u> means—

A looking for a job

B offering someone a job

C a person's regular job

D able to hold a good job

TEKS 5.2A

10 What effect did the moon landing have on the theme of this play?

F Watching the moon landing helped the country be brave.

G The moon landing caused the sisters to change in surprising ways.

H The moon landing reminded the sisters about the importance of family.

J The moon landing helped the family learn to work together.

TEKS 5.3C

Name _____ Date _____

**Read this selection. Then answer the questions that follow it.
Fill in the circle of the correct answer on your answer document.**

Teachers Belong in the Classroom

1   In an age when computers seem to have taken over the world, do
we really need teachers in classrooms? After all, there are software
programs that can teach us just about anything. There are programs
for learning a language and for solving math problems. There are
online courses that teach students at home. There are many tools for
learning without the help of human beings. So, do we need rooms with
desks and chairs? Do we really need teachers?

2   I believe that the answer is a firm "Yes!" Let's look first at the role of
the teacher. A teacher is not a machine that stores information. A
good teacher does far more than that. Having knowledge is important,
of course. Teachers go to school for many years. They must pass
difficult tests before they enter a classroom. They also work in the
classrooms of experienced teachers before they get their own
classrooms. We all expect a teacher to know the main <u>subjects</u>.
However, that is just the beginning.

69

3   Good teaching is an art. Think of the best teacher you ever had. What was special about that person? Did he or she know exactly which material to review with students? Seem to know when some students were feeling confused about a lesson? Or make a subject come alive and turn printed words into drama? Yes, it takes a great deal of understanding and patience to lead a classroom. Without a real teacher, a classroom is just a room.

4   Now, think about that room for a moment. Consider all the things that happen inside those four walls. Before lessons begin, students talk excitedly together about all the topics that interest them. They form friendships, gather in groups, and share news. Maybe they ask each other for some quick homework tips. Maybe they decide whom they will eat lunch with. Maybe they just exchange a quick smile with someone they would like to know better. These are the social moments of school that take place in the early hours of the day.

5   Then the teacher calls the class to order. It's time for learning. The night before, the students have read a short story or a chapter about history. Now it is time to talk about this homework. What did the author of the story really mean? What are the main ideas in the history chapter? The teacher may not tell you right away. The teacher wants you to think. He or she has a plan for helping you find your way through all those words! You have many of the clues already. The lesson is a map to help you find your way to some answers—and some interesting questions of your own. Another student makes a comment or a suggestion about the text. Maybe you raise your hand and offer some ideas. Whew! All that reading is beginning to make sense. It's fun to make those connections!

6   Now consider what would happen if you sat alone for six hours in an empty room. In front of you is a computer screen. Words and images appear on the screen, and a voice speaks to you. You can look at these words and pictures for as long as you like. No one is telling you to think, to hurry, to take part in a discussion. Nobody will say, "Sorry, but that isn't the answer I was waiting for." You can eat a sandwich while you tap on the keyboard. You can listen to music or answer the telephone. You can pretend there are other people around you.

GO ON

Grade 5: Reading Practice

7   But isn't it a little lonely in that room? Where are the other students? It seems as if you are floating in outer space. What happened to that lively conversation, those different voices adding to the buzz of the classroom? Hey, where *is* the classroom? Could it be that you actually miss school?

8   So let's go back to the lively classroom. There is your teacher, drawing a chart on the board, pointing out the <u>significant</u> words in a chapter. There is your teacher, moving around the room, stopping to help students who are stuck on a writing project. Students are told, "Write about something that is really important to you." You think, "Would anyone care about what is really important to *me*?" Your teacher does. He or she smiles at you, and suddenly, you feel like writing your own special story. Everyone else is writing, too. There is a faint hum in the room, the sound of minds at work. It is the sound of a real classroom.

1 The author of this selection probably believes that students—

A can help each other learn

B should sit quietly at their desks

C can learn nothing from computers

D should expect teachers to know everything

TEKS 5.12A

2 In paragraph 2, the word <u>subjects</u> means—

F groups of words that form part of a sentence

G someone or something studied in an experiment

H people who are under the rule of a king or queen

J courses of study in various branches of knowledge

TEKS 5.2B

3 One thing computerized instruction and classroom learning have in common is that they both—

A provide lively social relationships

B help students learn information

C give personal attention to students

D recognize when students are confused

TEKS 5.12A

4 In paragraph 7, which sentence stretches the truth to make a point?

F But isn't it a little lonely in that room?

G Where are the other students?

H It seems as if you are floating in outer space.

J Could it be that you actually miss school?

TEKS 5.12B

5 In paragraph 8, the word <u>significant</u> means—

A difficult

B important

C powerful

D puzzling

TEKS 5.2B

6 The reader can conclude that—

F schools will not be needed in the future

G schools serve students in many ways

H teachers should be better trained

J teachers expect too much of students

TEKS RC-5(D)

Grade 5: Reading Practice

7 Look at the cause-effect chart below.

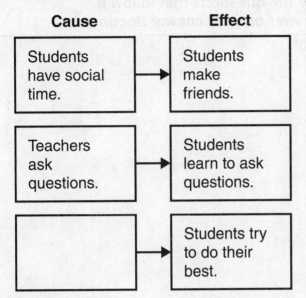

Cause   **Effect**

| Students have social time. | → | Students make friends. |

| Teachers ask questions. | → | Students learn to ask questions. |

| | → | Students try to do their best. |

Which sentence belongs in the blank box?

A Teachers study hard for years.

B Teachers plan their lessons.

C Teachers get classroom experience.

D Teachers encourage students.

TEKS 5.12A

8 Look at the thesaurus entry for the word comment.

> Main entry: **comment**
> **Synonyms:** criticism, illustration, remark, report

Which word could best replace comment as it is used in paragraph 5?

F Criticism

G Illustration

H Remark

J Report

TEKS 5.2E

9 Why does the selection compare computerized instruction to classroom instruction?

A To show the value of human teachers

B To show how education might change

C To suggest that schools should change

D To suggest that people learn in different ways

TEKS 5.11E

STOP

73

Read this poem. Then answer the questions that follow it.
Fill in the circle of the correct answer on your answer document.

Baseball

by Bill Zavatsky

1   We were only a farm team
    not "good enough" to
    make big Little League
    with its <u>classic</u> uniforms,
5   deep lettered hats.
    But our coach said
    we *were* just as good,
    maybe better,
    so we played
10 the Little League champs
    in our stenciled tee shirts
    and soft purple caps
    when the season was over.
    What happened that afternoon
15 I can't remember—
    whether we won or tied.
    But in my mind I lean back
    To a pop-up hanging
    In sunny sky,
20 stopped,
    nailed to the blue,
    losing itself in a cloud
    over second base
    where I stood waiting.
25 Ray Michaud, who knew,

Grade 5: Reading Practice

GO ON

my up-and-down career
as a local player,
my moments of graceful genius,
my unpredictable <u>ineptness</u>,
30   screamed arrows at me
from the dugout
where he waited to bat:
"He's gonna drop it! He
don't know how to catch,
35   you watch it drop!"
The ball kept climbing
higher, a black dot,
no rules of gravity, no
brakes, a period searching
40   for a sentence, and the sentence read:
"You're no good, Bill.
You won't catch this one now;
You know you never will."
I watched myself looking up
45   and felt my body rust, falling
in pieces to the ground,
a baby trying to stand up,
an ant in the shadow of a house.
I wasn't there—
50   had never been born,
would stand there forever,
a statue squinting upward,
pointed out, laughed at
for a thousand years
55   teammates, forgotten,

Reading
PRACTICE

TEKS 5.2B, 5.2E, 5.4, 5.8,
RC-5(D), RC-5(E)

anyone who played baseball
forgotten,
baseball forgotten, played no more,
played by robots on electric fields
60　who never missed
or cried in their own sweat.
I'm a lot older now.
The game was over
a million years ago.
65　All I remember
of that afternoon
when the ball
came down
is that
70　I caught it.

1 Read this dictionary entry for the word classic.

> **classic \klaʼ-sik** *Noun* **1.** a book or painting of the highest quality *Adjective*. **2.** of the best quality; excellent **3.** relating to ancient Greece or Rome **4.** always in fashion

Which definition most closely fits the way the word classic is used in line 4 of the poem?

A Definition 1

B Definition 2

C Definition 3

D Definition 4

TEKS 5.2E

2 In lines 19–20, the poet uses the words *sunny sky, stopped* to—

F create a pattern of sounds

G create a pattern of rhyme

H compare two similar things

J describe his mood at the time

TEKS 5.4

3 Which words help the reader understand what ineptness in line 29 means?

A *up-and-down career*

B *local player*

C *waited to bat*

D *"He's gonna drop it!"*

TEKS 5.2B

4 In line 38, the words *no rules of gravity* mean the—

F pitcher broke the rules

G ball kept on rising

H ball was lost forever

J players forgot the rules

TEKS RC-5(D)

5 Look at this web of imagery from the poem.

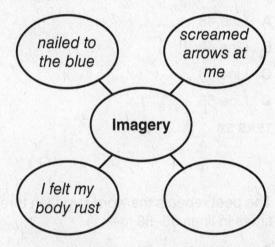

Which group of words best completes the web?

A *our stenciled tee shirts*

B *a statue squinting upward*

C *You know you never will*

D *I'm a lot older now*

TEKS 5.8

6 How does the poet feel while the ball is in the air?

   F Confident

   G Hopeless

   H Cheerful

   J Stubborn

TEKS RC-5(D)

7 In which line is the poet using figurative language to make a comparison?

   A Line 48

   B Line 49

   C Line 53

   D Line 55

TEKS 5.8

8 The poet repeats the word <u>forgotten</u> three times in lines 55–58 to—

   F explain that he cannot really remember the game fully

   G describe what happened during the game

   H predict what will one day happen to the game of baseball

   J show how long this part of the game seemed to him

TEKS 5.4

9 Which of the following is the best summary of this poem?

   A The poet remembers how nervous he felt while waiting for what seems like forever to catch a baseball during an important game. Even though he thinks he will fail, the poet catches the ball.

   B The poet is named Bill. Long ago, he played a game of baseball against a better team with good uniforms. The poet hopes he will not drop the ball. He thinks he will laugh if he does not catch it.

   C The poet recalls a game of long ago. Waiting and waiting, the ball seems to take forever to drop, giving the poet time to feel sorry for himself. However, he astonishes himself by catching the ball, which is something he is still proud of.

   D The poet wishes his team were as good as the Little League team. One hot summer day, the speaker waits at second base to catch a pop-up. He does not think that he will be able to make the catch, and that worries him. One of his teammates yells out that he is sure to drop the ball.

TEKS RC-5(E)

Name _____ Date _____

Reading
PRACTICE

TEKS 5.2B, 5.2E, 5.11A,
5.11E, 5.13A, 5.13B, RC-5(D),
RC-5(E), RC-5(F)

**Read the next two selections. Then answer the questions that follow them.
Fill in the circle of the correct answer on your answer document.**

Mae Jemison

by Elizabeth Raum

1   *As a girl in Chicago, Mae Jemison dreamed about spaceflight. After she graduated from medical school, that dream began to come true.*

2   In 1985, Dr. Jemison returned to Los Angeles to practice medicine. She attended school in the evenings to study biomedical engineering. Even though she was busy working as a doctor and studying, she had not forgotten her dream to travel into space. In October she filled out an application to enter NASA's astronaut training program. So did 2,000 other people.

3   In the early days of space flight, all the astronauts had been military pilots. By the 1970s, NASA realized that they also needed scientists, called mission specialists, to travel into space. Mission specialists help with the day-to-day running of the space shuttle, and they also work on science experiments. Some of the mission specialists were women, and some were African-American men. But there were no African-American women astronauts. Dr. Jemison hoped to become the first.

4   In June 1987, Dr. Jemison learned that she was one of fifteen people chosen to begin astronaut training. NASA officials asked her not to tell anyone until the next day when it would be announced on the news. Jemison was too excited to keep the secret. She told her cat, Sneeze, that they would be moving to Houston to begin astronaut training. Sneeze didn't tell anyone else.

5   Dr. Jemison moved to Houston and began a year of training. She learned all about the space shuttle and the history of flight. She took classes in meteorology, geology, and astronomy. She learned scuba diving, wilderness survival, and parachute jumping. Dr. Jemison hoped to become a mission specialist who would perform science experiments, so she learned all she could about day-to-day life on the shuttle.

GO ON

Name _____ Date _____

Reading
PRACTICE

TEKS 5.2B, 5.2E, 5.11A,
5.11E, 5.13A, 5.13B, RC-5(D),
RC-5(E), RC-5(F)

6   The astronaut trainees learned about weightlessness by flying in a
special jet, the KC-135. The airplane would fly high and then suddenly
drop down. For 20 to 30 seconds, the trainees would float through the
air just like they would on a real shuttle mission. It gave them a
chance to practice moving, eating, drinking, and working on the
equipment without <u>gravity</u> holding them down.

7   Dr. Jemison became an astronaut in August 1988. As a mission
specialist, Dr. Jemison began work at the Johnson Space Center. She
spent a year helping with other shuttle missions while she waited for
one of her own. In 1989, she was assigned to the newest space
shuttle, *Endeavour*. Her mission, *STS-47 Spacelab J,* was due to go
into space in September 1992. Dr. Jemison spent her time training
with six other members of the crew. Dr. Jemison and the *STS-47* crew
boarded the *Endeavour* on September 12, 1992. When it blasted into
space, Mae Jemison smiled! She loved the feeling of weightlessness
and didn't feel sick at all.

Grade 5: Reading Practice

Name _____ Date _____

Reading
PRACTICE

TEKS 5.2B, 5.2E, 5.11A,
5.11E, 5.13A, 5.13B, RC-5(D),
RC-5(E), RC-5(F)

8   Dr. Jemison spent her days in space working on science experiments. One tested a new way of helping astronauts deal with space sickness. Another studied the way people's bones change in space. She did experiments with frog eggs to see if they could develop in zero gravity. The astronauts worked twelve-hour shifts. When she was not sleeping or working, Dr. Jemison looked out the shuttle windows at the Earth, the Moon, and the stars.

9   *STS-47 Spacelab J* made 127 orbits of Earth and flew for 8 days. It landed on September 20, 1992. Friends and family were waiting to welcome Dr. Jemison home. Newspaper, television, and radio reporters asked her questions. She shared her excitement about the space flight. On Dr. Jemison's 36th birthday, the city of Chicago held a six-day celebration in her honor. She spoke at her old high school and told the students to follow their dreams.

Collecting Stardust

by John C. Waugh

The twenty-sixth of April, 1803, was a memorable date in the history of astronomy. On that day, a meteorite struck near L'Aigle in northern France, leaving thousands of easily collected fragments on the ground. Before then, people who claimed rocks fell from the sky were thought to be a little crazy, but after L'Aigle, meteorite investigation became respectable. Scientists have since found rocks that they suspect came from the Moon, from Mars, from the asteroid belt, and from the tails of comets. But tiny meteorites are much more

Grade 5: Reading Practice

Name _____ Date _____

Reading
PRACTICE

TEKS 5.2B, 5.2E, 5.11A,
5.11E, 5.13A, 5.13B, RC-5(D),
RC-5(E), RC-5(F)

common—about twenty tons of "micrometeorite dust" fall to Earth every day. Here's how you can get your hands on some of that stardust.

What You'll Need:

magnet
plastic bag
white paper
magnifying glass or microscope

What to Do:

1. Place magnet inside plastic bag. This will be your micrometeorite collector.

2. Take the collector outside to a bare patch of ground and drag it through the dirt. (Micrometeorites can be found anywhere outdoors, but rain will help collect ones that have fallen on roofs. The water washes the particles into gutters, so a good place to look is around the bottoms of gutter pipes.)

3. Once there are a lot of particles clinging to the outside of the plastic bag, turn it inside out. Now, though your magnet is still clean, you've got a collection of possible micrometeorites.

4. Go back inside and shake the particles out of the bag onto the white sheet of paper. Not all magnetic particles are micrometeorites. Many are flakes of rust from nails, sheet metal, and other construction materials. Examine the particles with a magnifying glass or microscope and separate the ones that look like flat flakes or chunks with sharp edges. These are probably rust. Since micrometeorites have nearly been burned up through friction with the air, they should appear to have been melted. Some will be smooth and almost spherical, and others will be lumpy but with rounded corners.

Save your best specimens in plastic bags or in clear plastic "bug boxes," or glue them to white cardboard. Your whole collection of stardust, billion-year-old souvenirs from space, may end up to be smaller than a postage stamp!

Grade 5: Reading Practice

Name _____ Date _____

Reading
PRACTICE

TEKS 5.2B, 5.2E, 5.11A,
5.11E, 5.13A, 5.13B, RC-5(D),
RC-5(E), RC-5(F)

Use "Mae Jemison" to answer questions 1–4.

---

1 Which information from paragraph 5 tells what Dr. Jemison will do on the space mission?

  A Dr. Jemison moved to Houston for a year of training.

  B Dr. Jemison took classes in meteorology, geology, and astronomy.

  C Dr. Jemison learned scuba diving and other outdoor skills.

  D Dr. Jemison planned to perform science experiments on the shuttle.

TEKS 5.11A

2 Which words from paragraph 6 help the reader understand what <u>gravity</u> means?

  F *fly, high*

  G *trainees, mission*

  H *practice, equipment*

  J *weightlessness, float*

TEKS 5.2B

3 You can tell that mission specialists are often—

  A experts in a particular field of science

  B people who have attended medical school

  C people who have always wanted to be astronauts

  D astronauts who have completed many space missions

TEKS RC-5(D)

4 Which of the following is the best summary of the selection?

  F Mae Jemison always wanted to be an astronaut, but when she got the chance, she only told her cat Sneeze about her new job. It was a very exciting time in her life. She did not feel sick at all on the flight. When she returned to Earth, she was honored by the city of Chicago.

  G Mae Jemison had always dreamed of exploring outer space. Her background in medicine and special training gained her a place on a NASA space mission. Jemison was thrilled to join the crew of the *Endeavour* in 1992 as a mission specialist. It was a dream come true.

  H Mae Jemison was a doctor who wanted to fly on a real shuttle mission. She got the chance in August 1988. She practiced on an airplane to get used to weightlessness. Jemison helped with other shuttle missions and then blasted off on the space shuttle, *Endeavour*. She did many experiments in space.

  J Mae Jemison, a fine doctor, was assigned to the newest space shuttle, *Endeavour*. She trained with six other astronauts. She worked with frog eggs during the flight into outer space. When she was not working or sleeping, Jemison gazed out the shuttle windows. She and the others worked twelve-hour shifts. It was a wonderful time in Jemison's life.

TEKS RC-5(E)

GO ON ▶

Use "Collecting Stardust" to answer questions 5–7.

5 Refer to step 4 of the directions for collecting stardust. Why is it important to use a white sheet of paper when you shake the particles out of the plastic bag?

A So the particles do not get on the furniture in your house

B So you will be able to see the shapes of the particles you found

C So you can clean off the magnet you used to gather the metal particles

D So the plastic bag can be emptied and used again

TEKS 5.13A

6 Read this dictionary entry for the word examine.

> **examine \ig-za-mən\ v. 1.** to study or analyze **2.** to check the health of **3.** to determine the health of **4.** to question formally

Which definition most closely fits the way the word examine is used in step 4?

F Definition 1

G Definition 2

H Definition 3

J Definition 4

TEKS 5.2E

7 Look at the table below.

Sources and Composition of Meteorites

Chondrites (stony meteorites)	Achondrites (stony meteorites)
Are made of the same material that formed the planets	Are made of material broken away from a larger heavenly body (asteroid, planet)
Come from heavenly bodies that never melted	Come from the outer crust of a larger heavenly body that melted and separated into layers of inner and outer crust and core
Are rich in minerals and elements such as iron and magnesium	Are rich in minerals and elements such as iron and magnesium

What can scientists most likely tell from examining a meteorite?

A Which layer of a heavenly body it came from

B What minerals and elements it is made of

C Which type of heavenly body it came from

D All of the above

TEKS 5.13B

GO ON

Name _____ Date _____

Reading
PRACTICE

TEKS 5.2B, 5.2E, 5.11A,
5.11E, 5.13A, 5.13B, RC-5(D),
RC-5(E), RC-5(F)

Use both "Mae Jemison" and "Collecting Stardust" to answer questions 8-10.

---

8 Read the diagram below and answer the question that follows.

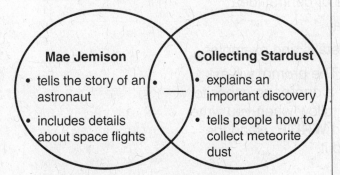

Mae Jemison
- tells the story of an astronaut
- includes details about space flights

Collecting Stardust
- explains an important discovery
- tells people how to collect meteorite dust

Which information applies to both selections?

F Celebrates the achievements of a famous person

G Tells about topics related to outer space

H Describes a procedure that readers can follow

J Explains the importance of having goals in life

TEKS RC-5(F)

9 Mae Jemison would probably be most interested in—

A collecting meteorite dust

B visiting the asteroid belt

C visiting L'Aigle in northern France

D meeting people who have stardust collections

TEKS 5.11E

10 Based on both of these selections, you can tell that—

F only highly trained people can study outer space

G there were no important discoveries in astronomy before 1803

H it takes a lot of work to become a mission specialist at NASA

J our knowledge of space has changed over the past two hundred years

TEKS 5.11E

Grade 5: Reading Practice

Name _____ Date _____

Writing a One-Page Composition

Responding to a Prompt

Do you ever write in a journal? Do you use email? Do you write reports for school? You probably answered *yes* to at least one of these questions. If so, you know that people use writing every day. That is why it is important to know how to write well. Writing well means:

- Focusing on one personal experience or central idea
- Organizing your writing in a logical way
- Developing your ideas with specific details and examples

On a test, you will be given a writing prompt. The prompt will ask you to write a one-page personal narrative or a one-page expository composition. The prompt will include rules to follow when you write. These rules are **READ** or **LOOK, THINK,** and **WRITE.** Read the prompt carefully to make sure you understand it.

Step 1: Plan Your Composition

It is very important to organize your ideas before you start writing. Think about these examples:

- A prompt asks you to write a one-page personal narrative about an important event in your life. On a separate sheet of paper, you can draw a web such as the one at right. First write the important event in the center circle. Then list ideas and details about the event in the other circles. Decide which details to keep, and cross out the rest. Once you finish your web, you are ready to write a first draft of your personal narrative. Always keep in mind that your composition can be no longer than one page.

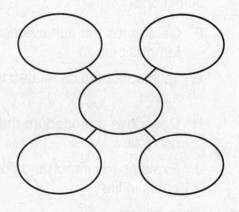

- Another prompt asks you to write a one-page expository composition explaining how to do something. You can use a flowchart such as the one at right. At the top of the flowchart, write a topic sentence to establish your **central idea.** Then list each step or detail in your explanation in the boxes of the flowchart. Make sure your steps follow a logical order and connect to your central idea. Now, you are ready to write a first draft of your expository composition.

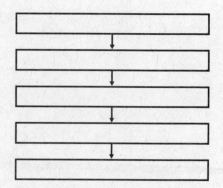

Grade 5: Writing

Step 2: Draft Your Composition

You can use the ideas in your graphic organizer to write a first draft. Your composition should have a clear beginning, middle, and ending. Develop your ideas by using specific details and well-chosen examples. This will make your composition interesting to read. Be sure to reread the writing prompt and check that you have responded to it correctly.

Step 3: Revise and Edit Your Composition

Reread your draft to make sure that you have responded correctly to the writing prompt. Then, look for ways to improve your writing. For example:

- As you reread your personal narrative, look for sentences that do not focus on the important event you wrote about. Delete sentences that do not tell about that event, and add sentences that do.

- As you reread your expository composition, delete or rewrite sentences that do not support the central idea. Check that every fact, detail, and explanation is specific and connects to the central idea. Make sure that you have a strong concluding statement at the end of your composition.

- For each type of composition, ask yourself questions like these:

  - Does every sentence have a purpose? If not, delete or rewrite it.

  - Is every sentence in the best place? If not, consider moving it around.

  - Does my writing seem choppy? Think about varying the lengths of the sentences.

  - Does my writing flow smoothly? Is it easy to understand? If not, consider where you could add transition words, such as *next, then, as a result,* to connect your ideas clearly.

- When you are writing a one-page composition, every sentence counts and every word counts. Look again at your word choices. Replace overused words with words that are more interesting and descriptive. Delete any words that are not necessary.

- Now check your draft for errors in language conventions. Correct errors in spelling, grammar, capitalization, and punctuation. Errors like these can distract and confuse readers.

- **Your final draft should include all of the changes you made.** Write neatly so readers can understand every word. Make sure your composition is no longer than one page.

Grade 5: Writing

Name _____ Date _____

Written Composition: Personal Narrative

TEKS 5.15B, 5.15C, 5.15D, 5.17

READ

Read the story in the box below.

> David wanted to earn his camp certificate for swimming. He was the only camper in his cabin who did not have the certificate yet. The problem was that he was afraid to swim with his head underwater. To face his fears, David practiced each morning at the pool. On the last day of camp, David swam the length of the pool—underwater. It was the bravest thing he had ever done.

THINK

Think of something you have done that you were afraid to do.

Then think about how you acted bravely to face your fears.

WRITE

Write a one-page personal narrative about the bravest thing you have ever done.

As you write your composition, remember to —

❏ describe a personal experience—a time when you acted with courage.

❏ develop your composition with details that will help the reader understand your experience and your feelings.

❏ look for ways to rearrange or delete sentences in order to improve transitions.

❏ use correct spelling, capitalization, punctuation, grammar, and sentences.

❏ make sure your composition is no longer than one page.

Tip
Before writing, list important events in the order they happened. Use this list to organize the ideas in your composition.

Tip
Make sure each word is well chosen and each sentence serves your purpose.

Name _____ Date _____

Sample Response: Personal Narrative

> **Write a one-page personal narrative about the bravest thing you have ever done.**

The writer begins by getting the reader's attention and introducing the topic.

Would you feel relaxed climbing 50 feet into the air? I sure didn't but had the courage to try. Our class took a trip to the Alpine Tower. This is a 50-foot climbing thing made of telephone poles. It looks like a giant X with ropes and nets hanging off of it. I remember standing next to it wondering if I would make it to the top.

Before you start climbing you have to put on a harness and a helmet and be hooked to a rope. A man on the ground is hooked to the same rope and he keeps you from falling. I remember my heart beating very fast when I started to climb. My teacher and friends were on the ground watching me and helping me see places to put my feet and hands so I could climb higher.

The writer includes details that describe her experience and her feelings.

I got half way up and stopped because I was really scared. It felt like I was frozen and I couldn't make myself move another inch. I decided to come down. I was happy for myself because I tried at least. The kids who made it all the way up said there was something secret at the top. I hope we go again next year. Maybe I'll be brave enough to see what's up there.

Grade 5: Personal Narrative

Name _____ Date _____

Sample Response: Personal Narrative

> **Write a one-page personal narrative about the bravest thing you have ever done.**

<table>
<tr>
<td>

The writer needs to show clear transitions between ideas, sentences, and paragraphs.

</td>
<td>

The bravest thing I have ever done is go to a new school. It was so hard for me to fall asleep the night before school started my stomach hurt. In the morning my eyes look sleepey. I went to the kitchen to eat my cereal and almost fell asleep in it. Snap! That's so crazy.

</td>
</tr>
</table>

My mom drove me to school. My bus is usally number 14. We went to the school office and then she left. All the students were there in the classroom. They starred at me when I walked in and my stomach started to hurt. The teacher said my name to the class and that I was a new student. She told me where to sit. I don't remember to much about my first day of school but I was nervous.

<table>
<tr>
<td>

The writer needs concluding sentences that explain how she felt at the end of the first day.

</td>
<td>

I have friends in my new school like Milly and Alicia. They are just like friends at my old school because we laugh and play jokes sometimes.

</td>
</tr>
</table>

Grade 5: Personal Narrative

Name _____ Date _____

Written Composition: Personal Narrative

READ

Read the story in the box below.

> Luz was just walking into school when she remembered she had not done her math homework. She felt worried enough to speak to her teacher about the problem. Her teacher suggested that she work on the homework during recess and even offered to help her. Luz gratefully accepted the offer, completed the math problems, and handed in her work. She promised herself to write down her assignments in the future.

THINK

Think of a day when you forgot to do something important. Then think about what happened as a result.

WRITE

Write a one-page personal narrative about a time when you forgot to do something important.

As you write your composition, remember to —

❑ think about a personal experience—a time when you forgot to do something important.

❑ organize your ideas into a clear beginning, middle, and end.

❑ develop your composition with details that will help the reader understand your experience and your feelings.

❑ use correct spelling, capitalization, punctuation, grammar, and sentences.

❑ make sure your composition is no longer than one page.

Tip
Before writing, decide how you will organize the events in your composition.

Tip
When you have finished your draft, look for simple sentences that can be combined to make your writing smoother.

91

Sample Response: Personal Narrative

> **Write a one-page personal narrative about a time when you forgot to do something important.**

| The writer organizes the narrative so that the order of events is clear. |

About two months ago was the last time I remember forgetting to do something important. That day was busy. I felt like I had so many things to do and remember. I had homework after school and soccer practice too. My team was practicing extra that week for the C-2 Tri-County tournament.

The thing that I forgot was to talk to my grandma on the phone and say happy birthday. The day after her birthday, I was just talking to Darryl and Chance after soccer practice when that terrible thought came to my head. I saw what I did and then that was all I could think about on the ride home. I was nervous to call her because I felt so bad. She never forgets to call me on my birthday but I forgot hers. Missing a birthday is a terrible mistake because it's only special on that one day.

| The writer includes an ending that wraps up the story and touches on the topic again. |

When I talked to Grandma on the phone I felt better. She was laughing and said not to worry about it. She did not sound even a little bit sad. She said she's had a lot of birthdays and she said she was happy to talk to me. I hope I never never forget Grandma's birthday again.

Sample Response: Personal Narrative

> **Write a one-page personal narrative about a time when you forgot to do something important.**

The writer includes details that do not support the main idea.

The writer does not punctuate dialogue correctly, which could confuse the reader.

One time I forgot to feed the nabors cat for a whole day. The Deckers next door asked me to feed their cat on the weekend because they were driving out of town. I said I would no problem. They wanted me to fill up the cat food bowl and water bowl in the morning on Saturday and Sunday.

I did a good job Saturday morning. Sunday night at dinner we were having spaghetti. My mom said, Did you remember to feed the cat this morning? I said Oh no! My mom was not happy. It was getting dark but I went to the Deckers house and the cat started MEOWing really loud. He was probably hungry. His bowls were empty. When I got home my mom said that I had to say to the Deckers what happened.

Written Composition: Expository

TEKS 5.15B, 5.15C, 5.15D, 5.18A(i), 5.18A(ii), 5.18A(iii), 5.18A(iv)

READ

Read the quotation in the box below.

> **"Throw off the bowlines, sail away from the safe harbor. Catch the trade winds in your sails. Explore. Dream. Discover." – Mark Twain**

THINK

Mark Twain, whose real name was Samuel Clemens, was a steamboat pilot on the Mississippi River before he became a famous author. In this quotation, attributed to Mark Twain, he gives some valuable advice.

Think of a distant place you would like to explore. Then, think about why you would enjoy exploring it.

Tip
Begin by introducing your central idea in a way that grabs your audience's attention.

WRITE

Write a one-page expository composition that explains why you would like to explore a particular place.

Tip
Use a variety of sentence structures to make your writing more interesting.

As you write your composition, remember to —

❑ think about the central idea—a place you would like to explore, and why.

❑ organize your composition so that the key ideas are clear to your audience.

❑ develop your central idea using facts, details, and explanations.

❑ use correct spelling, capitalization, punctuation, grammar, and sentences.

❑ make sure your composition is no longer than one page.

Name _____ Date _____

Sample Response: Expository

> **Write a one-page expository composition that explains why you would like to explore a particular place.**

The writer puts the central idea in the first paragraph.

If I could explore a place it would be outer space. What an exciting and dangerous place that would be! I have to say I would be pretty scared at times but it would be worth it. Who knows where you might land or what aliens you might find.

The first reason I would go is to be the first person to go past where everyone else has already gone. Someone has to because that is how we get deeper and deeper into space. I want to be the first person to stand on a planet and see 5 moons in the sky. It would also be cool to be the first person to high five an alien.

Paragraphs have a topic sentence and supporting sentences that give clear details or explanations.

The second reason would be to find things to bring back to Earth. Maybe I could bring back something that makes sick people get better or makes sad people happy. All the technolgy from the aliens could make our lives better. Maybe the good thing I find is a planet where some people from Earth could live so it is not so crowded here.

When I get back from space they would probably have a parade for me after they checked me for outer space diseases. I would be a good example to other people because I was willing to travel away and come back to tell everyone about it.

Grade 5: Expository

Sample Response: Expository

> Write a one-page expository composition that explains why you would
> like to explore a particular place.

> The composition sounds choppy because there is not enough sentence variety.

I have seen pictures of Hawai on TV and that is the place I want to explore. When I see a picture of Hawai I want to be there right away. A boat or a plane could take me there. Hawaii looks very beautiful it has beautiful beaches and tropicle flowers and animals.

I want to explore Hawai because it looks very different from where I live and it is warm all the time. There are hula dancers that wear grass skirts. There are volcanos to explore to. I would also want to eat the different food there. I want to swim in the ocean.

> The writer does not provide a concluding sentence.

Exploring Hawai would take a lot of time because there are many islands. I don't even know all the names of them. I would have to take a boat or plane to get to other islands. I wonder if each island looks different or if they look the same.

Written Composition: Expository

READ

Read the story in the box below.

> Oscar was new to gymnastics class. Maria explained to him, step by step, how to do a cartwheel. She described it so well that Oscar was able to do one that day.

THINK

Think of something you do well. Then think about how to tell someone else how to do it.

Tip

Before you begin writing, list the steps you would use to show what you do well.

WRITE

Write a one-page expository composition that explains how to do something that you do well.

As you write your composition, remember to —

❏ think about the central idea—something you do well.

❏ develop the idea using steps in a process and supporting facts, details, or explanations.

❏ use transitions to link paragraphs.

❏ use correct spelling, capitalization, punctuation, grammar, and sentences.

❏ make sure your composition is no longer than one page.

Tip

Write a concluding paragraph that encourages your readers to try something new.

Sample Response: Expository

> **Write a one-page expository composition that explains how to do something that you do well.**

Taking care of my dog is something I do very well. This is because I have had a lot of practice. It is also because I love my dog so much. It's pretty easy when you get the hang of it. Let me tell you how.

> The writer supports the central idea with examples and explanations.

Dogs need to go outside to use the bathroom. My dog comes in my room and pushes my arm with her nose. This lets me know she needs to go out. Now comes the gross part. I have to pick up after her with a plastic bag and put it in the trash so the yard stays clean. This is the WORST part of taking care of a dog.

But wait! There are great parts to taking care of a dog too. Like feeding her once a day. I like this part because my dog gets so happy and excited at dinner. She gets three cups of food a day because she is a pretty big dog. She also gets some snacks during the day but not too many.

> The writer uses transition words or phrases to link paragraphs.

Another great part is playing with her and walking her. Find out what your dog likes to do, like playing with a ball or running after a stick, and do that with your dog as much as you can. My family takes turns walking our dog at least a half hour a day and that seems to be the right amount.

Finally, the easiest part of taking care of a dog is petting her and talking to her. If you do all these things you and your dog will be very happy and also very good friends!

Sample Response: Expository

> **Write a one-page expository composition that explains how to do something that you do well.**

The writer does not organize the steps of this process in a clear way. ⊳

The meaning of this sentence is not clear because of spelling errors and confusing wording. ⊳

Here is how you catch a fly ball. You need a baseball glove that goes on your hand you don't throw with. Keep your eye on the ball that is coming at you. Now, you mite want to close your eyes when the ball is coming at your face but don't do it.

Hold the glove top up if the ball is coming above your belt. Hold the glove top down like a basket if the ball is going to go below your belt. You stand to catch the ball with your feet a little bit apart and your knees a little bit bent. Oh what I all mos forgot stand so you are going a little bit at the ball like on you're toes.

You want to catch the ball with both hands. The hand with no glove on it goes next to your glove and goes over the end of your glove when you catch the ball. Now maybe the ball won't pop out. Remember what I said and you can catch a fly ball.

TEKS 5.15B, 5.15C,
5.15D, 5.17

Written Composition:
Personal Narrative

READ

Read the story in the box below.

> Chris had never wanted to take music lessons. The idea of spending a beautiful day practicing an instrument bored him. Because his grandmother gave him her piano, Chris's parents signed him up for lessons. Strangely enough, Chris began to enjoy his new ability to play scales and simple pieces. Often, the hours would fly by as he worked on his fingerings and developed his ear for music.

THINK

Think of something you changed your mind about and what caused this change. Then think about what you discovered through this experience.

WRITE

Write a one-page personal narrative about a time you changed your mind about something.

As you write your composition, remember to —

❏ think about a personal experience—a time when you changed your mind about something.

❏ organize your composition in order of events.

❏ develop your composition with details that explain how the experience changed your ideas.

❏ keep your purpose and audience in mind.

❏ use correct spelling, capitalization, punctuation, grammar, and sentences.

❏ make sure your composition is no longer than one page.

Name _____   Date _____

Written Composition: Personal Narrative

READ

Read the story in the box below.

> Megan was watching her favorite television show when the doorbell rang. Her neighbor Laurie was in tears because she couldn't find her kitten. Megan agreed to go with Laurie and search the house and yard for Tilly, the lost pet. The two girls hunted throughout the house until a mewing noise from the attic told them where the kitten had wandered. Laurie was so happy and relieved to find her pet, and Megan felt good about helping someone to solve a problem.

THINK

Think of a time when someone needed your help with a problem. Then think about what it was like to help him or her.

WRITE

Write a one-page personal narrative about a time when you helped someone to solve a problem.

As you write your composition, remember to —

❏ think about a personal experience—a time when you helped someone to solve a problem.

❏ decide how you will organize your composition.

❏ develop your composition by sharing thoughts about this problem and how it was solved.

❏ keep your audience and purpose in mind.

❏ use correct spelling, capitalization, punctuation, grammar, and sentences.

❏ make sure your composition is no longer than one page.

101

Written Composition: Expository

TEKS 5.15B, 5.15C, 5.15D, 5.18A(i), 5.18A(ii), 5.18A(iii), 5.18A(iv)

READ

Read the passage in the box below.

> The Model T car gave the average American the opportunity to own a vehicle. The refrigerator gave us a way to preserve foods that would otherwise spoil. The computer changed the way we work and play.

THINK

Think of an invention that has changed life for the better. Then think about how this invention benefits people.

WRITE

Write a one-page expository composition explaining how an important invention has improved people's lives.

As you write your composition, remember to —

❏ think about the central idea—how an important invention has improved people's lives.

❏ organize your ideas so that your audience will understand them.

❏ include an introduction and a concluding paragraph.

❏ develop your key ideas using facts, details, and explanations.

❏ use correct spelling, capitalization, punctuation, grammar, and sentences.

❏ make sure your composition is no longer than one page.

Name _____ Date _____

Written Composition

TEKS 5.15B, 5.15C,
5.15D, 5.18A(i), 5.18A(ii),
5.18A(iii), 5.18A(iv)

Written Composition: Expository

READ

Read the paragraph in the box below.

> Some people are good role models. We look up to them because they have qualities we admire. They might be leaders in a particular field who fill their lives with interesting activities. Often, they do exciting things or lead the way in the arts or sciences, or in sports.

THINK

Think about a person from the past or present with whom you would like to change places.

WRITE

Write a one-page expository composition that explains why you would like to change places with a person whom you admire.

As you write your composition, remember to —

❏ think about the central idea—why you would like to trade places with this person.

❏ organize your composition so that key ideas are clear to your audience.

❏ develop your central idea using language and examples that your audience will understand.

❏ use a variety of sentences and transitions.

❏ use correct spelling, capitalization, punctuation, grammar, and sentences.

❏ make sure your composition is no longer than one page.

Name _____ Date _____

Revising

After you have finished the first draft of a composition, you still have work to do. The next step is **revising**. Revising means fixing problems in your writing such as parts that do not make sense or ideas that are out of order. Revising includes adding, deleting, and moving text.

When you revise a paper, you can delete details or sentences that you do not need, and you can add or move details and sentences to better support the main idea. You can also make sure that you have used simple, compound, and complex sentences correctly and that you have written with the audience in mind.

Read this chart to learn more about ways to revise your writing.

Check
• Make sure all of the examples, facts, and details that you included help the reader understand your topic or main idea.

Add
• Add transition words such as *after, then,* and *because*.

Delete
• Delete words, sentences, and paragraphs that are not about the main idea.
• Delete facts that do not give information about the main idea, even if they are interesting.

Move
• Move a word, sentence, or paragraph if it would fit better in another part of the paper.

Sentences
• Use a variety of simple, compound, and complex sentences.
• When possible, combine related ideas into one sentence.

> **Read the introduction and the passage below. Then read each question.**
> **Fill in the circle of the correct answer on your answer document.**

Elana started writing this passage about the custom of potluck. She needs help revising it. Read her composition and think about the changes she should make. Then answer the questions that follow.

Potluck, Anyone?

(1) "Potluck" used to mean food provided for a guest who was not expected. (2) The guest had to take "the luck of the pot." (3) That meant eating whatever the host happened to have in the kitchen. (4) That could be good luck—or bad!

(5) Later, the term came to mean something different. (6) She invites some friends. (7) She tells each guest to bring a tasty dish. (8) One brings a salad or a vegetable dish. (9) Another might bring sandwiches or chili or dessert.

(10) That is one reason these meals are quite popular. (11) Another is that nobody has to work too hard in the kitchen. (12) Instead, the cooks share the work and maybe even their favorite family recipes.

> **Tip**
>
> The main idea should be clearly stated at the beginning of a passage.

> **Tip**
>
> Think about the writer's use of sentences and how she could add variety.

Name _____ Date _____

TEKS 5.15C, 5.18A(i),
5.18A(ii), 5.18A(iii),
5.18A(iv)

1 Which sentence could **BEST** be added before sentence 1?

A Preparing a big meal can take a lot of work.

B Potluck dinners are not always very good.

C Many people enjoy sharing meals with friends.

D People have enjoyed potluck meals for centuries.

TEKS 5.18A(i)

Tip
Try each sentence before sentence 1.

2 Which sentence could be added before sentence 5?

F The term "potluck" goes back to the 16th century.

G One time there was a potluck dinner on my block.

H A casserole is a meal that you can cook in one pot.

J It is not the same thing as a Native American potlatch.

TEKS 5.18A(iii)

3 Which transitional sentence can connect the ideas in sentences 5 and 6?

A I would usually rather go to a restaurant.

B Imagine that your mom decides to host a potluck dinner.

C A potluck dish should feed at least ten people.

D The more people who come, the more food there is.

TEKS 5.15C

Tip
Think about the flow of the sentences in the passage. Find the sentence that sounds best in that place.

4 Which revision correctly combines sentences 6 and 7?

F She invites some friends until she tells each guest to bring a tasty dish.

G She invites some friends, she tells each guest to bring a tasty dish.

H She invites some friends, and she tells each guest to bring a tasty dish.

J Because she invites some friends, she tells each guest to bring a tasty dish.

TEKS 5.15C

GO ON

5 Which sentence could **BEST** follow sentence 9 to add sentence variety?

A Another might bring a stew or casserole.

B One might invite a friend.

C Just imagine all the food choices at a potluck!

D Another might volunteer to bring drinks.

TEKS 5.18A(iv)

6 Which of the following is a good concluding sentence for this composition?

F A community can have fun gatherings where people get to know one another.

G Kids can help out in the kitchen, too.

H The potluck is quite a popular tradition, and there are usually a lot of leftovers.

J A potluck lets guests and hosts enjoy good food and each other's company.

TEKS 5.18A(ii)

Read the introduction and the passage below. Then read each question. Fill in the circle of the correct answer on your answer document.

Mark started writing this story about a sleepover at a friend's home. He needs help revising it. Read his story and think about the changes he should make. Then answer the questions that follow.

A Great Sleepover

(1) Arturo's family lives in a tall wooden house on a shady street. (2) His front yard is full of bicycles and balls and toys because there are five children in the family. (3) I knew I was going to have fun when the front door opened and his brothers and sisters came running out into the yard.

(4) When the sun was starting to go down, Arturo's mom called us in for dinner. (5) Late in the afternoon, we all played catch outside. (6) That was one of the best meals I ever had: enchiladas, rice, tortilla chips, and a spicy dip. (7) For dessert, Arturo's dad brought out a pudding with caramel sauce. (8) That made Arturo's parents smile at me.

(9) Right away, Arturo introduced me to the whole family, then showed me around their large house. (10) Each room was painted a different color. (11) Everyone had a definite idea about the best color for a bedroom. (12) Arturo's room was dark blue. (13) Arturo's room had a jungle scene on one wall. (14) You probably think lions are interesting animals.

Grade 5: Revising Practice

© Houghton Mifflin Harcourt Publishing Company

(15) The next morning, we drove to a lake about twenty miles away. (16) The sun was shining. (17) It wasn't hot. (18) Arturo's dad put bait on our hooks, and we sat on the rocks, waiting for a bite. (19) I thought I was never going to catch anything, but then the line went tight and I pulled in a bass. (20) What a great weekend!

---

1 Which sentence should be added before sentence 1?

A Arturo Fuentes and I are in the same class this year.

B Arturo's mother often gives me a ride home from school.

C Just yesterday, I thought about calling Arturo's parents to say thanks.

D Last Saturday, I stayed over at my friend Arturo's house for the first time.

TEKS 5.15C

2 What is the **BEST** place to move sentence 4?

F After sentence 5

G After sentence 6

H After sentence 7

J After sentence 8

TEKS 5.15C

3 What is the correct place to move the second paragraph?

A Before the first paragraph

B After the first paragraph

C After the third paragraph

D After the fourth paragraph

TEKS 5.15C

4 Which sentence could **BEST** follow sentence 7?

F I liked the yellow rice, too.

G Arturo likes chocolate best.

H When I saw it, I grinned.

J Mrs. Fuentes set the table.

TEKS 5.15C

Grade 5: Revising Practice

© Houghton Mifflin Harcourt Publishing Company

5 Which revision correctly combines sentences 12 and 13?

A Arturo's room was dark blue, on one wall there was a picture of a jungle scene.

B Arturo's room was dark blue, and it had a picture of a jungle scene on one wall.

C Arturo's room was dark blue, also on one wall there was a picture of a jungle scene.

D Arturo's room was dark blue, or on one wall there was a picture of a jungle scene.

TEKS 5.15C

6 Which sentence does **NOT** belong in the third paragraph?

F Sentence 11

G Sentence 12

H Sentence 13

J Sentence 14

TEKS 5.15C

7 What is the **BEST** way to combine sentences 16 and 17?

A The sun was shining, and it wasn't hot.

B The sun was shining, but it wasn't hot.

C The sun was shining, because it wasn't hot.

D The sun was shining, for it wasn't hot.

TEKS 5.15C

8 Which sentence could **BEST** follow sentence 19 to add precise details?

F Drop lines are also good for fishing.

G The fish shack in town sells lunch foods.

H Before we left, we found some bugs for bait.

J By late afternoon, we had four big bass in the cooler.

TEKS 5.15C

Grade 5: Revising Practice

Name _____ Date _____

**Read the introduction and the passage below. Then read each question.
Fill in the circle of the correct answer on your answer document.**

---

*Madison started writing this article about a new park in her town. She needs
help revising it. Read her article and think about the changes she should make.
Then answer the questions that follow.*

Park Opening on Saturday

(1) Every town should have a park where people can have fun. (2) The new park will have a playground, a baseball field, a basketball court, and a picnic area.

(3) Two years ago the city made plans to make the park better. (4) Finally the work is finished. (5) Now kids from Fairfield School will have a place to play during recess and after school. (6) Miss Olivera said she will take her PE classes to the park to play baseball, kickball, and basketball. (7) The park is a great place for everyone in the city to go in the summer.

(8) The playground now has slides, swings, and a seesaw. (9) There is a sandbox for the younger kids, too. (10) The most exciting thing about the playground is the climbing wall. (11) The wall is very hard to climb. (12) There is a climbing wall at a nearby amusement park.

(13) The new field has lights so teams can play at night. (14) The baseball field will be ready just in time for the start of the summer season. (15) Fans will like the new seats, too. (16) There is also a snack bar that will sell food and drinks during the games. (17) The snack bar is something that everyone will like!

(18) My brother and his friends are so excited about the new basketball court. (19) Until now they have been playing on our driveway. (20) Both teams must shoot the

Name _____ Date _____

ball at the same basket. (21) Players are looking forward to playing on a full court with a basket at each end.

(22) In fact, hundreds of people are expected to use the park before opening day. (23) The mayor will cut the ribbon at noon. (24) My parents and I want to arrive early. (25) Mr. Howard, the director of the Fairfield Parks Department, will give a welcome speech. (26) Then there will be a free throw contest, baseball games, and sack races.

---

1 Which sentence could BEST be added after sentence 1 to introduce the topic?

A Our park has been closed a long time.

B I enjoy playing baseball in the park.

C People walk their dogs and push baby strollers in the park.

D This Saturday, May 15, the Fairfield Memorial Park will reopen.

TEKS 5.18A(iii)

2 Which sentence could BEST be added after sentence 2 to include a fact about the park?

F In the summer, there will also be wading pools for younger children.

G A lot of people will really enjoy these changes to the park.

H The park has the best playground ever.

J Our park should have big sports fields.

TEKS 5.18A(iii)

3 Which topic sentence should be added to the third paragraph?

A Miss Olivera's class can play field sports in the park.

B The work on the town park began two years earlier.

C The park is a good place for students.

D The city has added new equipment.

TEKS 5.18A(ii)

4 Which sentence does NOT belong in the third paragraph?

F Sentence 9

G Sentence 10

H Sentence 11

J Sentence 12

TEKS 5.15C

GO ON

Grade 5: Revising Practice

Name _____ Date _____

Revising
PRACTICE

TEKS 5.15C, 5.18A(i),
5.18A (ii), 5.18A(iii),
5.18A(iv)

5 Which sentence could **BEST** be added after sentence 16?

   A I do not think the snack bar will serve pizza.

   B My favorite snacks are popcorn and fruit punch.

   C The snack bar will not have as many choices as the cafeteria.

   D Visitors to the park often get hungry and thirsty.

   TEKS 5.18A(iii)

6 Which sentence is the **BEST** transition between sentence 21 and the next paragraph?

   F All members of school teams will get new uniforms because citizens have donated money for them.

   G Many players are coming to practice on the courts, even though the park has not officially opened yet.

   H While there are two dog runs in the new park, dogs are not allowed on the playing fields.

   J Most people in our community feel that the money spent on fixing up the park has been well spent.

   TEKS 5.18A (iv)

7 Which sentence could **BEST** be added after sentence **24**?

   A That way, we will be able to see and hear the speakers.

   B The mayor is going to run for his second term in office soon.

   C In the late afternoon, people will help clean up the park.

   D The park is usually not too crowded on weekday mornings.

   TEKS 5.15C

8 Which sentence could **BEST** conclude the article?

   F I hope it will not rain and spoil all the wonderful plans.

   G The fifth-graders decided not to hold a bake sale at the park.

   H The opening of Fairfield Park is an event that no one in the community should miss.

   J You do not have to participate in these events, if you don't like games very much.

   TEKS 5.18A(i)

Grade 5: Revising Practice

Editing

TEKS 5.15D, 5.20A, 5.20B, 5.20C, 5.21A, 5.21B, 5.21C, 5.22A, 5.22B, 5.22C, 5.22D

Editing is one of the final stages in the writing process. When you edit your writing, you read it carefully to look for errors in grammar, punctuation, capitalization, and spelling. The goal of editing is to catch and correct your errors, especially those that may distract or confuse your readers.

Read this chart to learn more about ways to edit your writing.

Grammar

- Make sure that you have used collective nouns, verbs, adjectives, adverbs, and prepositional phrases correctly.

- Check that sentences have complete subjects and complete predicates.

- Be sure that simple, compound, and complex sentences have correct subject-verb agreement.

Punctuation and Capitalization

- Make sure that you have used quotation marks to show someone's exact words.

- Check that you have used commas correctly in compound sentences.

- Be sure to capitalize abbreviations, initials, acronyms, and organizations' names.

Spelling

- Check that you have correctly spelled words with silent and sounded consonants.

- Check that you have correctly spelled words with Greek and Latin roots and suffixes.

- Check that you have correctly spelled commonly confused words, such as *its* and *it's*.

Grade 5: Editing

Editing

TEKS 5.15D, 5.20A, 5.20B, 5.20C, 5.21A, 5.21B, 5.21C, 5.22A, 5.22B, 5.22C, 5.22D

Read the introduction and the passage below. Then read each question. Fill in the circle of the correct answer on your answer document.

Jose started writing this essay about his father. He needs help editing it. Read the essay and think about the changes he should make. Then answer the questions that follow.

A Person I Admire: My Dad

(1) When I think about the people I admire, my dad is the first one who comes to mind. (2) He is an EMT, which stands for emergency medical technician. (3) His job includes many responsibilities. (4) The most important one is to help people when they have phisical injuries.

Tip
Remember to capitalize abbreviations.

(5) EMT's have to be brave because they sometimes face challenging situations. (6) My dad has helped unconscious people and sometimes has perform CPR. (7) He has helped save drivers on highways and bridges. (8) He has even gone out during powerful storms to rescue people. (9) Many people see my father as a hero but he is very modest. (10) He believes he is simply doing his job.

Tip
Check to see that both the complete subject and the complete predicate are written correctly.

(11) While training for his job, Dad learned many skills. (12) When someone suddenly stops breathing, he can help. (13) If a person has a heart attack or stroke, Dad takes action immediately. (14) It's not surprising that he got the better

GO ON

Grade 5: Editing

test scores of all his classmates in the training program.

(15) Although my dad doesn't take hisself too seriously, Mom and I are proud of him.

---

1 What change, if any, should be made in sentence 2?

A Change *EMT* to **emt**

B Delete *which*

C Change *technician* to **technicien**

D Make no change

TEKS 5.21A(i)

2 What change should be made in sentence 4?

F Change *help* to **helps**

G Insert a *comma* after **people**

H Change *have* to **had**

J Change *phisical* to **physical**

TEKS 5.22B(ii)

3 What change, if any, should be made in sentence 6?

A Change *perform* to **performed**

B Change *CPR* to **cpr**

C Change *sometimes* to **some times**

D Make no change

TEKS 5.20C

4 What change should be made in sentence 9?

F Change *people* to **peoples**

G Insert a comma after *hero*

H Change *very* to **a lot**

J Change *modest* to **moddest**

TEKS 5.21B(i)

Tip
A compound sentence is made up of two shorter sentences joined by a comma and a conjunction.

GO ON ➡

Grade 5: Editing

5 What change should be made in
sentence 14?

A Change *surprising* to **surprise**

B Change *better* to **best**

C Change *of* to **under**

D Insert a comma after *classmates*

TEKS 5.20A(iii)

6 What change, if any, should be made in
sentence 15?

F Change *Although* to **All though**

G Change *hisself* to **himself**

H Change *I* to **me**

J Make no change

TEKS 5.15D

Editing
PRACTICE

TEKS 5.15D, 5.20A(iv),
5.20A(vi), 5.20C, 5.21B(ii),
5.21C, 5.22B(iv), 5.22C

> **Read the introduction and the passage below. Then read each question.**
> **Fill in the circle of the correct answer on your answer document.**

Connor started writing this article about a food drive. Read Connor's article and look for corrections and improvements he should make. Then answer the questions that follow.

Food Drive

(1) The fifth grade is holding a canned food drive next week. (2) We are helping to collect food for the Lincoln Food Bank. (3) Our food drive is part of our school's Community Service Month. (4) As Principal Green says, You are never too young to serve your community."

(5) In January, each class works on a community service project. (6) The fifth grade is working on helping people who do not have enough money for food. (7) Last month, we read the book Hunger in America to learn about this serious problem. (8) We learned about the millions of people in our country whose refrigerators are nearly empty. (9) We also discovered that many people don't get enough of the vitamins they need to stay healthy. (10) Many families struggle to afford nutritious foods, such as fruits and vegetables. (11) Any people know that to go hungry for even one day is a painful condition.

(12) Hunger effects many families in our own town. (13) We discovered that even more families go hungry in

GO ON

© Houghton Mifflin Harcourt Publishing Company

the winter because they have to pay for heat as well as groceries. (14) December, January, and February can be dificult months for many families unless we help. (15) That's why, for the final week of January, we are collecting food for people in our community. (16) Food from our cupboards will go to local shelters and the homes of the elderly.

(17) We are encouraging people to look through their cupboards for cans for donatiun. (18) Often, students bring in two, three, or more cans of food for our drive. (19) You bring the food, and we delivering it! (20) We look forward to seeing you at our food drive.

---

1 What change should be made in sentence 4?

A Change *Principal* to **principal**

B Delete the comma after *says*

C Insert a quotation mark before *You*

D Change the period to a question mark

TEKS 5.21B(ii)

3 What change, if any, should be made to sentence 11?

A Change *Any* to **Many**

B Change **hungry** to **hunger**

C Change *day* to **days**

D Make no change

TEKS 5.20A(vi)

2 What change should be made in sentence 7?

F Delete the comma after *month*

G Change *read* to reading

H Underline *Hunger in America*

J Change *this* to **these**

TEKS 5.21C

4 What change, if any, should be made in sentence 12?

F Insert a comma after *Hunger*

G Change *effects* to **affects**

H Change *families* to **families'**

J Make no change

TEKS 5.22C

GO ON

Grade 5: Editing Practice

5 What change should be made in sentence 14?

A Change *January* to **Janruary**

B Change *months* to **monthes**

C Change *dificult* to **difficult**

D Change *we* to **we're**

TEKS 5.15D

6 What change should be made in sentence 17?

F Change *are* to **were**

G Change *through* to **threw**

H Change *their* to **they're**

J Change *donatiun* to **donation**

TEKS 5.22B(iv)

7 What change, if any, should be made in sentence 18?

A Change *Often* to **Oftener**

B Delete the comma after *three*

C Change *more* to **most**

D Make no change

TEKS 5.20A(iv)

8 What change should be made in sentence 19?

F Change *You* to **You'd**

G Change *bring* to **brings**

H Change *delivering* to **deliver**

J Change *it* to **them**

TEKS 5.20C

Name _____   Date _____

Editing
PRACTICE

TEKS 5.20A(i), 5.20A(v),
5.20A(vii), 5.20A(viii),
5.21A(iii), 5.22A(i),
5.22B(i), 5.22D

Editing

> **Read the introduction and the passage below. Then read each question.**
> **Fill in the circle of the correct answer on your answer document.**

Rita started writing this story about a birthday surprise.
She needs help editing it. Read her article and think
about the changes she should make. Then answer the
questions that follow.

The Loan

(1) Did you ever wish people wouldn't borrow things from you? (2) When you have a little sister, you end up loaning them your clothes, toys, and books a lot. (3) Sometimes, it's forever although you get your things back. (4) Sometimes, however, you get more than you expected.

(5) That day, my six-year-old sister Emma asked if she could borrow my rain boots with the pink and yellow flowers. (6) I said that it wasn't raining and that the boots were too big for her feet. (7) She smiled and said that didn't matter, promising to give them back soon. (8) I autamatically shrugged and went back to my book. (9) I figured Emma and her friends were playing dress up, and I was busy planning a report about the World Health organization.

(10) An hour later, Emma came back. (11) Now she asked to borrow my favorite coat. (12) This was becoming <u>annoyying</u>, but I knew she would keep bugging me if

Name _____ Date _____

Editing
PRACTICE

TEKS 5.20A(i), 5.20A(v),
5.20A(vii), 5.20A(viii),
5.21A(iii), 5.22A(i),
5.22B(i), 5.22D

I said no. (13) However, I told her not to get it dirty, and she ran off with the coat, her red pigtails flying behind her.

(14) Soon I grown hungry for a snack, so I went downstairs to the kitchen. (15) There was Emma, bent over the counter doing something with a huge sheet of paper. (16) The boots and coat were on the floor in a pile. (17) Knowing the coat would need a careful inspectshon, I began to reach for it. (18) Emma turned and begged me to leave the room, so I shook my head, grabbed an apple, and left.

(19) The next morning, my bedroom door was covered with an amazing life-size drawing of me in my favorite coat and rain boots. (20) The words "Happy Birthday" were drawn neatly of the picture. (21) I ran to find Emma and give her a hug. (22) I found out she gave me a lot more than she borrowed.

---

1 What change, if any, should be made in sentence 3?

A Change *although* to **until**

B Change *get* to **got**

C Change *your* to **you're**

D Make no change

TEKS 5.20A(vii)

2 What change, if any, should be made in sentence 8?

F Change *autamatically* to **automatically**

G Change *shrugged* to **shrug**

H Insert a comma after *and*

J Make no change

TEKS 5.22B(i)

GO ON

Grade 5: Editing Practice

Editing
PRACTICE

TEKS 5.20A(i), 5.20A(v),
5.20A(vii), 5.20A(viii),
5.21A(iii), 5.22A(i),
5.22B(i), 5.22D

3 What change should be made in sentence 9?

A Change *were* to **was**

B Delete the comma after *up*

C Change *report* to **rapport**

D Change *organization* to **Organization**

TEKS 5.21A(iii)

4 Which set of dictionary guidewords would help you to find the correct spelling of the underlined word in sentence 12?

F amusement, anchor

G anthill, anyplace

H animal, annual

J attraction, authority

TEKS 5.22D

5 What change should be made in sentence 13?

A Change *However* to **Therefore**

B Delete the comma after *dirty*

C Change *ran* to **run**

D Change *flying* to **flew**

TEKS 5.20A(viii)

6 What change should be made in sentence 14?

F Change *Soon* to **Then**

G Change *grown* to **grew**

H Delete the comma after *snack*

J Insert a comma after *downstairs*

TEKS 5.20A(i)

7 What change, if any, should be made in sentence 17?

A Change *would* to **wood**

B Change *careful* to **carful**

C Change *inspectshon* to **inspection**

D Make no change

TEKS 5.22A(i)

8 What change should be made in sentence 20?

F Change *Birthday* to **birthday**

G Delete the quotation marks

H Change *drawn* to **drawed**

J Change *of* to **below**

TEKS 5.20A(v)

123

Texas Write Source
Assessments

Name _____ Date _____

Pretest

Part 1: Basic Elements of Writing

> **Questions 1–12:** Read each sentence. Choose the best way to write the underlined part of the sentence. Fill in the circle of the correct answer on your answer document.

1 The <u>childrens names</u> are Tori and Ray.

   A childs' names

   B children's names

   C childrens' names

   D Make no change

2 The students <u>spoke quiet</u> as they worked in the library.

   F speak quiet

   G spoken quietly

   H spoke quietly

   J Make no change

3 These are the <u>fresher tomatoes</u> I have ever seen.

   A freshest tomatoes

   B fresh tomatoes

   C fresh tomato

   D Make no change

4 Our house is <u>near the train station</u>.

   F at the train station

   G in the train station

   H between the train station

   J Make no change

5 The new mall <u>will opened</u> next month.

   A was open

   B were open

   C will open

   D Make no change

6 Rico <u>jumped carefully</u> over the wooden fence.

   F jumped careful

   G jump carefully

   H jumps careful

   J Make no change

7 Kathy will make salad <u>either</u> cole slaw for the school picnic.

   A but

   B or

   C for

   D Make no change

8 Millie and Shani decided to ride <u>their</u> bicycles to school.

   F theirs

   G they

   H her

   J Make no change

Name _____ Date _____

9 Last week, I <u>invite</u> members of the computer club to meet at my home.

  A invited

  B invites

  C will invite

  D Make no change

10 She painted her room a <u>cheerfuller yellow</u>.

  F a cheer yellow

  G a cheerfullest yellow

  H a cheerful yellow

  J Make no change

11 <u>My aunt are</u> a wonderful cook.

  A My aunt be

  B My aunt is

  C My aunt were

  D Make no change

12 Every weekend, my sister and I <u>hikes</u> through Smugglers' Notch.

  F hiking

  G hike

  H is hiking

  J Make no change

Questions 13–18: Read each question and fill in the circle of the correct answer on your answer document.

---

13 Which is the best way to combine these two sentences?

> Jan likes to play video games.
>
> José likes to play video games, too.

  A Jan and José likes to play video games.

  B Video games are played by Jan and José.

  C Jan likes and José likes to play video games.

  D Jan and José like to play video games.

14 Which is the best way to combine these two sentences?

> The girls rented bicycles.
>
> The girls rode to the beach.

  F The girls rented bicycles but rode to the beach.

  G The girls rented bicycles and rode to the beach.

  H The girls rode to the beach, then rented bicycles.

  J The girls rented bicycles and the girls rode to the beach.

Texas Write Source Assessments

Name _____ Date _____

15 Which is an interrogative sentence that should end with a question mark?

   A Rain forests cover only 2 percent of the earth's surface

   B When people cut down the trees, they destroy the rain forests

   C After people cut down the trees, what do they use the land for

   D Many types of plants and animals live in the world's rain forests

16 Which is an exclamatory sentence that should end with an exclamation point?

   F I can't believe I ate that whole pizza

   G Some pizzas have thin crusts

   H Can a pizza be cooked in a microwave oven

   J Pizza is a popular food in the United States

17 Which is a complete sentence written correctly?

   A The Erie Canal, begun in 1817.

   B Connected Lake Erie and the Hudson River.

   C The Erie Canal took eight years to build.

   D Transport products between eastern and western United States

18 Which pair of sentences uses the best transition to connect ideas?

   F It was cold. On the other hand, I wore my hat.

   G It was cold. Next I wore my hat.

   H It was cold. On top of it, I wore my hat.

   J It was cold. Therefore I wore my hat.

GO ON

Questions 19–20: A student wrote this paragraph about working at the local food bank. It may need some changes or corrections. Read the paragraph. Then read each question. Fill in the circle of the correct answer on your answer document.

Helping Out

On Friday my father and I went to the Disaster Relief Center. The center gives groceries to victims of hurricanes or other disasters who have no food. We did several jobs there. We sorted all the cans of food that people gave to the center. Then we put together boxes of food for the families. We packed up rice, cereal, and canned vegetables and fruit. Finally we helped load all the boxes onto trucks. We finished at about 4:00, and then we jogged home through the park.

19 What type of paragraph is this?

A narrative

B descriptive

C persuasive

D response to a text

20 Which sentence is the topic sentence of the paragraph?

F We did several jobs there.

G On Friday my father and I went to the Disaster Relief Center.

H We packed up rice, cereal, and canned vegetables and fruit.

J We finished at about 4:00, and then we jogged home through the park.

GO ON

Name _____ Date _____

Part 2: Proofreading and Editing

Questions 21–30: Read the passages. Choose the best way to write each underlined part. Fill in the circle of the correct answer on your answer document.

Today in class we learned about symbols. Our teacher said, "A symbol is

anything that stands for something else." For example a white dove is a
                    21   22

symbol for piece. A heart stands for love. Mr parker asked us to look for symbols
              23   24

as we walked home. I saw a metal sign with a picture of a bus. That told me the

location of a bus stop. As I walked past the beach, I saw a sign showing a dog in

a circle with a line drawn through it. That symbol means dogs are not

allowed on the beach. I realized that we are surrounded by symbols.
       25

21 A "A symbol is anything that stands for something else."

   B A symbol is anything that stands "for something else."

   C 'A symbol is anything that stands for something else.'

   D Make no change

22 F for example

   G For example;

   H For example,

   J Make no change

23 A peace

   B peice

   C pease

   D Make no change

24 F mr. Parker

   G Mr. Parker

   H mr parker

   J Make no change

25 A That symbol means dogs are not allowed on the beach?

   B That symbol means dogs are not allowed on the beach!

   C That symbol means dogs are not allowed on the beach,

   D Make no change

GO ON

Name _____ Date _____

Dear Kisha:
26

   I love my vacation in Florida. The <u>whether</u> is sunny and warm,
                                        27

and I'm having a great time. My <u>grandmothers house</u> is near the water. <u>Gran</u>
                                  28

<u>and</u> I go to the beach almost every day. I love looking for shells. I am going to
29

show them to the <u>science Club</u> in school. Wait until you see them! I even found
                   30

a starfish and a large sand dollar! Maybe next year you could come with me.

   Wouldn't it be fun to look for shells together?

   I'll call you when I get home.

                                         Your friend,

                                         Amy

26 F Dear Kisha,

   G Dear Kisha

   H Dear Kisha;

   J Make no change

27 A Weather

   B whither

   C weather

   D Make no change

28 F Grandmothers

   G Grandmother's

   H grandmother's

   J Make no change

29 A Gran and us

   B Me and gran

   C Gran and me

   D Make no change

30 F Science club

   G science club

   H Science Club

   J Make no change

GO ON

Name _____ Date _____

Part 3: Writing   Narrative

READ

The difference between children and adults is that adults are responsible for themselves. They no longer depend on their parents for a home, for food, and for money. To feel more grown-up is to feel you are becoming more adult or responsible.

THINK

What have you done recently that made you feel you are growing up? Think about what happened and why or how it made you feel that way.

WRITE

Write a narrative composition telling something you did recently that made you feel more grown-up or responsible.

As you write your composition, remember to —

❏ focus on one thing you did that made you feel more grown-up

❏ organize your ideas in an order that makes sense, and connect the ideas with transitions

❏ develop your ideas with specific details

❏ make sure your composition is no longer than one page

Name _____ Date _____

Progress Test 1

Part 1: Basic Elements of Writing

Questions 1–12: Read each sentence. Choose the best way to write the underlined part of the sentence. Fill in the circle of the correct answer on your answer document.

---

1 For many years in the United States, some <u>people was</u> not allowed to vote.

   A people were

   B people are

   C people is

   D Make no change

2 Native Americans, African Americans, and women <u>had to waited</u> many years before they could vote.

   F had to waiting

   G had to wait

   H have to waited

   J Make no change

3 In the 1800s, women <u>beginned to speak</u> out about the right to vote.

   A began to speak

   B begins to speak

   C beginning to speak

   D Make no change

4 Many people believed that letting women vote was a <u>dangerously</u> idea.

   F danger

   G dangerouser

   H dangerous

   J Make no change

5 In 1848, Elizabeth Cady Stanton and Lucretia Mott held a convention in New York to fight for <u>women's rights</u>.

   A womans rights

   B womens rights

   C womens' rights

   D Make no change

6 In 1870, African American men <u>final</u> gained the right to vote.

   F finaler

   G finally

   H finalist

   J Make no change

7 Southern states <u>quicker</u> passed laws to deny African Americans this right.

   A quickest

   B quick

   C quickly

   D Make no change

8 All voters had to pay an <u>unfair</u> poll tax before they could vote.

   F a unfair

   G a more unfair

   H an unfairer

   J Make no change

Name _____ Date _____

9 In 1924, Congress <u>passing</u> a law giving Native Americans voting rights.

  A passed

  B pass

  C was passing

  D Make no change

10 Today more people than ever <u>has</u> the right to vote.

  F had

  G have

  H is having

  J Make no change

11 Surprisingly, only about 55 percent of Americans <u>who</u> can vote actually do vote.

  A which

  B whose

  C whom

  D Make no change

12 By voting, they can help make decisions for <u>ourselves</u>.

  F them

  G itself

  H themselves

  J Make no change

Questions 13–18: Read each question and fill in the circle of the correct answer on your answer document.

---

13 Which is a complete sentence written correctly?

  A Playing a video game in the car.

  B Abel and the video club.

  C Members of the video club met at his house.

  D Abel with the newest computer game.

14 Which is a run-on sentence and should be written as two sentences?

  F Vijay takes his dog to the park every day.

  G The new park is great the dogs love it.

  H Jyoti likes to walk in the new park.

  J Vijay and Jyoti often walk the dog together.

15 Which is the best way to combine these two sentences?

> We play basketball at the playground.
>
> The playground is new.

  A We play basketball at the playground it is new.

  B We play basketball at the playground, the playground is new.

  C We play basketball at the playground, and the playground is new.

  D We play basketball at the new playground.

GO ON

Name _____ Date _____

16 Which is the best way to combine these two sentences?

> My aunt made oatmeal cookies.
> My aunt said I could eat some.

F My aunt made oatmeal cookies and my aunt said I could eat some.

G My aunt made oatmeal cookies and said I could eat some.

H My aunt made oatmeal cookies and I ate some of them.

J My aunt made oatmeal cookies but said I could eat some.

17 Which is an interrogative sentence that should end with a question mark?

A Does your aunt make chocolate chip cookies

B I like chocolate chip cookies best

C Ana Sofia's favorite cookie is peanut butter chip

D Gretchen says she would rather have an apple

18 Which is a declarative sentence that should end with a period?

F Is either Miguel or Tony good at baking

G Yikes, what a mess they left in the kitchen

H Miguel also bakes bread and muffins

J Can we ask Miguel and Tony to bake something for the party

Name _____ Date _____

Questions 19–20: A student wrote this paragraph about planting a garden. It may need some changes or corrections. Read the paragraph. Then read each question. Fill in the circle of the correct answer on your answer document.

---

(1) My mother says that the vegetables in the store are never fresh. (2) This year she decided to grow her own. (3) Of course, we had to help. (4) Then we had to dig up the earth. (5) First, we had to find a place in the backyard for a garden. (6) Next, we planted tomato seeds, beans, and squash seeds. (7) Two weeks later, my mother gave up. (8) The birds and squirrels had eaten every seed. (9) My mother now says that perhaps the vegetables in the store don't look so bad after all.

19 Which supporting detail could be added after sentence 1?

  A Squirrels also like to eat birdseed and nuts of all kinds.

  B She is tired of buying squishy tomatoes and cucumbers.

  C My sister doesn't like to garden.

  D We watered the garden every day.

20 Which two sentences should be switched to organize the paragraph better?

  F sentences 1 and 2

  G sentences 2 and 3

  H sentences 4 and 5

  J sentences 8 and 9

GO ON

Name _____ Date _____

Part 2: Proofreading and Editing

> **Questions 21–30: Read the passages. Choose the best way to write each underlined part. Fill in the circle of the correct answer on your answer document.**

Ava has a problem. Her friend Len's little dog barks all day while he is at

school. The constant barking is driving Ava's mother and her neighbors crazy.

"Ava, <u>your</u> Len's friend," said one neighbor. "He never puts that yappy dog
    21

in the <u>house: We</u> <u>here</u> that barking all day. Can't you say something to him?"
   22   **23**

Ava struggled with what to say to Len. Finally, she decided to tell him the

truth. When Len found out, <u>he</u> promised to keep the dog in during the day.
             24

"<u>Can solve</u> this problem. After all," he smiled, "if he needs more fresh air, I'll
  25

let him stay out all night instead!"

---

21 A you is

   B you're

   C you were

   D Make no change

22 F house. We

   G house? We

   H house, we

   J Make no change

23 A hear

   B hare

   C air

   D Make no change

24 F his

   G it

   H him

   J Make no change

25 A Can solving

   B We can solve

   C Them can solve

   D Make no change

GO ON →

Name _____ Date _____

I really like "The Adventures of Tom Sawyer" by Mark Twain. It is one
        26

of my favourite books. Tom lives with aunt Polly and his half-brother Sid in
    26   **28**

Mississippi! Tom's best friend is Joe Harper. Twain says they have "two souls
  29

but a single thought," which means they think alike.

   It was very exciting when Joe and Tom ran away to an island with Huck

Finn. They have a great time but everyone in town thinks they are dead. Tom
          30

even goes to his own funeral!

   Later, Tom and Becky Thatcher get lost in a cave. I won't tell you what

happens. You will have to read the book for yourself. I recommend that you do.

26 F *The Adventures of Tom Sawyer*

 G 'The Adventures of Tom Sawyer'

 H "the adventures of Tom Sawyer"

 J Make no change

27 A favorrite

 B favorite

 C fauvorite

 D Make no change

28 F aunt polly

 G aunt Polly

 H Aunt Polly

 J Make no change

29 A Mississippi?

 B Mississippi.

 C Mississippi:

 D Make no change

30 F time; but

 G time, but

 H time. But

 J Make no change

GO ON ➡

Part 3: Writing   Expository

READ

In the decimal system, numbers are based on multiples of 10—0.10, 1.0, 10, 100, 1000, and so on. The U.S. money system is based on the decimal system.

THINK

Think about how amounts of money more than $1 are written. How are amounts of money less than $1 written? How would you explain our money system to someone from another country?

WRITE

Write an expository composition explaining how the U.S. money system works.

As you write your composition, remember to—

❏ think about the focus of your composition—how our money system works

❏ organize your ideas in an order that makes sense, and connect the ideas with transitions

❏ develop your ideas with facts, details, and examples

❏ make sure your composition is no longer than one page

Progress Test 2

Part 1: Basic Elements of Writing

> **Questions 1–12:** Read each sentence. Choose the best way to write the underlined part of the sentence. Fill in the circle of the correct answer on your answer document.

1 Many kinds of animals live <u>by the pond</u>.

   A about the pond

   B for the pond

   C of the pond

   D Make no change

2 There are three types of rodents: squirrel-like rodents, mouse-like rodents, <u>but</u> cavy-like rodents.

   F and

   G so

   H or

   J Make no change

3 One type of cavy-like rodent <u>am</u> a guinea pig.

   A be

   B are

   C is

   D Make no change

4 Squirrels build winter nests called drays <u>for themselves</u>.

   F for theirselves

   G for ourselves

   H for itself

   J Make no change

5 Squirrels' nests <u>are maked</u> of sticks and leaves.

   A is made

   B are made

   C are making

   D Make no change

6 A squirrel's front teeth <u>continue to grow</u> throughout its life.

   F continued to grow

   G continue to grew

   H continuing to grow

   J Make no change

7 As squirrels jump, their bushy tails help <u>they</u> keep their balance.

   A it

   B him

   C them

   D Make no change

8 The American red squirrel is <u>smaller</u> than the gray squirrel.

   F more small

   G more smaller

   H smallest

   J Make no change

Name _____ Date _____

9 One of the cutest mouse-like rodents <u>are</u> the gerbil.

A be

B is

C were

D Make no change

10 Gray squirrels <u>oftenly share</u> their sleeping dens and winter nests to stay warm.

F often share

G oftener share

H very oftenly share

J Make no change

11 Can the American red squirrel jump <u>highest</u> than the gray squirrel?

A highly

B higher

C high

D Make no change

12 Squirrels are <u>cleverer</u> and determined rodents.

F cleverest

G most clever

H clever

J Make no change

GO ON

Name _____ Date _____

13 Which details best expand this sentence and make it more interesting?

> The light bulb burned out.

A The light bulb burned out, and we replaced it.

B With a harsh glow and a sudden loud pop, the light bulb burned out.

C As she turned on the switch, the light bulb burned out.

D She needs a new light bulb because the old bulb burned out.

14 How can this sentence best be expanded to make it more interesting?

> Kim and her sister got a kitten.

F Yesterday Kim and her sister got a kitten.

G Kim and her sister are happy they got a kitten.

H Kim got a kitten, and her sister got a kitten.

J Kim and her sister got a sweet calico kitten from the animal shelter.

15 Which is the best way to combine these two sentences?

> We can take the bus to the store.
> We can ride our bikes to the store.

A We can take the bus or ride our bikes to the store.

B We can take the bus to the store and ride our bikes.

C To the store we take the bus or ride our bikes.

D Take the bus or ride our bikes to the store.

16 In which sentence do the underlined pronoun and verb agree?

F <u>Someone have</u> extra tickets for the movie.

G <u>No one want</u> the movie tickets.

H <u>Everyone is</u> going to the concert instead.

J <u>All</u> of us <u>has</u> tickets for the concert.

GO ON

Name _____ Date _____

17 Which sentence shows an active voice?

   A The letter was written by Emily.

   B The dancing was done by the children.

   C The cat moved to the music.

   D The dancers were watched by the dog.

18 Which is the best way to combine these two sentences?

> We had fun ice skating. It was snowing all day.

   F We had fun ice skating, but it was snowing all day

   G Although it was snowing all day, we had fun ice skating.

   H After we had fun ice skating, it was snowing all day

   J It was snowing all day before we had fun ice skating.

Questions 19–20: A student wrote this paragraph about a class trip to the aquarium. It may need some changes or corrections. Read the paragraph and each question. Fill in the circle of the correct answer on your answer document.

A Class Trip

(1) Yesterday I went to the aquarium with my class. (2) We saw sharks, squid, a swordfish, and several types of fish I've never seen before. (3) Then we went to an outside pool and watched three incredibly smart dolphins perform. (4) I once saw dolphins on TV. (5) Later, we went into another building that had a large wave tank. (6) There we learned how waves are made and why tides occur. (7) It was a great trip!

19 What type of paragraph is this?

   A expository

   B persuasive

   C narrative

   D response to a text

20 Which sentence should be removed to improve this paragraph?

   F sentence 1

   G sentence 3

   H sentence 4

   J sentence 6

GO ON

Name _____ Date _____

Part 2: Proofreading and Editing

Questions 21–30: Read the passages. Choose the best way to write each underlined part. Fill in the circle of the correct answer on your answer document.

Every year the Caldecott Medal is awarded to the artist <u>which</u> has
21

illustrated "the most distinguished (famous) American picture book for

children." This award is named for Randolph Caldecott. He illustrated picture

books during the late 1800s. At the age of six, Caldecott showed a talent for

drawing. At 21, <u>studied</u> at the School of Art in <u>Manchester England</u>. Caldecott
22   23

drew the pictures for <u>alot</u> of children's books. However his best-known book
24

is <u>'The House That Jack Built.'</u>
25

21 A who

   B whose

   C whom

   D Make no change

22 F he studying

   G they studied

   H he studied

   J Make no change

23 A manchester England

   B Manchester, England

   C Manchester; England

   D Make no change

24 F a lot

   G alots

   H allot

   J Make no change

25 A "The House That Jack Built"

   B The House That Jack Built

   C *The House That Jack Built*

   D Make no change

GO ON ➡

Name _____ Date _____

Dear Tyrone,

Well, here I am in Houston. I came with my parents to visit our relatives.

Yesterday we went to the <u>johnson space Center</u> with my <u>twelve-year old</u>
                                   26   **27**

cousin. We took the <u>N.A.S.A.</u> Tram Tour. It was amazing! This weekend we
                        28

are going to the <u>Lyndon B Johnson</u> National Historical Park. We'll see where
                        29

President Johnson lived. I will show you pictures when we get home on <u>Sunday</u>
                                                                     29

Your friend,

Kayla

26 F Johnson space center

   G Johnson Space Center

   H johnson space center

   J Make no change

27 A twelve year-old

   B twelve year old

   C twelve-year-old

   D Make no change

28 F NASA

   G Nasa

   H *NASA*

   J Make no change

29 A Lyndon B. Johnson

   B Lyndon b Johnson

   C Lyndon b. Johnson

   D Make no change

30 F Sunday.

   G Sunday?

   H sunday!

   J Make no change

GO ON →

Part 3: Writing   Expository

READ

By now, you've studied many kinds of animals in your science classes. For example, you know a great deal about different kinds of birds, mammals, fish, reptiles, and amphibians, to name a few.

THINK

To compare two animals, you tell how they are alike. To contrast them, you tell how they are different.

WRITE

Write an expository composition that compares and contrasts two animals.

As you write your composition, remember to —

❏ compare and contrast two different animals

❏ organize the ideas in an order that makes sense, and connect the ideas with transitions

❏ develop your ideas with facts, details, and examples

❏ make sure your composition is no longer than one page

Name _____ Date _____

Post-test

Part 1: Basic Elements of Writing

> **Questions 1–12: Read each sentence. Choose the best way to write the underlined part of the sentence. Fill in the circle of the correct answer on your answer document.**

1 All of my friends <u>looks</u> forward to summer vacation.

   A is looking

   B look

   C looking

   D Make no change

2 Most of my <u>friend's families</u> like to visit national parks.

   F friend's family

   G friends' families

   H friends families

   J Make no change

3 Last week Kanye <u>telled</u> us about his trip to Yellowstone Park.

   A told

   B tell

   C telling

   D Make no change

4 Sara is going to Spain and will definitely enjoy <u>themselves</u>.

   F itself

   G herself

   H theirselves

   J Make no change

5 Of all the trips we have taken, this one is the <u>better</u>.

   A well

   B good

   C best

   D Make no change

6 The Grand Canyon was <u>more deep</u> than I had imagined.

   F deeper

   G deepest

   H most deep

   J Make no change

7 Vacations in the mountains are fun, <u>so</u> hiking can be exhausting.

   A but

   B if

   C for

   D Make no change

8 Juan says that one of his favorite places <u>are</u> Georgia.

   F be

   G is

   H were

   J Make no change

Name _____ Date _____

9 I was <u>total surprised</u> by how blue
the water is in the Gulf of Mexico.

   A total surprise

   B totally surprising

   C totally surprised

   D Make no change

10 Jing Mai <u>like to go</u> swimming
every morning.

   F like going

   G likes to go

   H like to goes

   J Make no change

11 Mr. Garcia spent two weeks camping
<u>in the desert.</u>

   A along the desert

   B on the desert

   C at the desert

   D Make no change

12 Esperanza travels <u>most often</u>
than Alex does.

   F very often

   G more often

   H oftener

   J Make no change

Questions 13–18: Read each question and fill in the circle of the correct answer on your answer document.

---

13 Which noun describes the underlined
words in the sentence below?

> Pete has <u>thirty special coins</u>.

   A batch

   B collection

   C cluster

   D bunch

14 Which is a run-on sentence and should
be written as two sentences?

   F We need to recycle more of our trash,
pollution affects our environment.

   G We recycle only about 14.1%
of our trash.

   H We burn 15.2% of the garbage and
pile tons of it in enormous heaps.

   J Unfortunately, 70.7% ends up
in the landfills.

15 Which is the best way to combine
these two sentences?

> Neil Armstrong became the first
> person to walk on the moon.
>
> He walked on the moon
> on July 20, 1969.

   A Neil Armstrong the first person to walk
on the moon on July 20, 1969.

   B On July 20, 1969, Neil Armstrong
became the first person to walk on
the moon.

   C On July 20, 1969, Neil Armstrong
walked on the moon first.

   D Neil Armstrong on July 20, 1969,
the first person to walk on the moon.

GO ON

Name _____ Date _____

16 Which is the best way to combine these two sentences?

> Abraham Lincoln was our sixteenth president. He was mostly self-educated.

F Abraham Lincoln, our sixteenth president, was mostly self-educated.

G Mostly self-educated, our sixteenth president was Abraham Lincoln.

H Self-educated Abraham Lincoln was our sixteenth president.

J Abraham Lincoln was self-educated, and was our sixteenth president.

17 Which is a declarative sentence that should end with a period?

A When was Lincoln elected president

B Have you read any of his speeches

C Read the speech right now

D His most famous speech is the Gettysburg Address

18 Which is an interrogative sentence that should end with a question mark?

F What time will the concert start

G I asked Sally if she wanted to go to the concert

H Sally is busy and will not go

J The concert starts at eight this evening

Questions 19–20: A student wrote this paragraph about the Triangle Shirtwaist fire. It may need some changes or corrections. Read the paragraph. Then read each question. Fill in the circle of the correct answer on your answer document.

The Triangle Shirtwaist Fire

On March 25, 1911, a fire broke out in the Triangle Shirtwaist Factory in New York City. This company made women's blouses, called "shirtwaists." No one knows how the fire started, but it spread quickly. Workers ran for the fire escape, but it collapsed. They tried the doors, but the owners had locked them. At least 146 people died in the blaze, mostly women and children. People were shocked by what happened. They forced the city to make strict fire safety laws.

19 What type of paragraph is this?

A narrative

B expository

C persuasive

D response to a text

20 Which detail sentence could best be added just before the last sentence?

F This tragedy made people care about workers' safety.

G The doors were locked so that workers couldn't steal clothing.

H A spark from a sewing machine may have started the fire.

J Workers on the ninth floor did not know there was a fire.

GO ON

Name _____ Date _____

Part 2: Proofreading and Editing

> **Questions 21–30:** Read the passages. Choose the best way to write each underlined part. Fill in the circle of the correct answer on your answer document.

One way to make your writing more <u>exsiting</u> is to use <u>similes?</u> A simile
               21   **22**

is a figure of speech that compares two things, using either like or as. For

example, you could write "The branches of the tree hit my window." But to

add imagery to your writing, try this: "The branches tapped at my window

like bony fingers." Famous boxer Muhammad Ali liked to use similes when <u>he</u>
                                         23

described how he fought in the ring. He once <u>said, " I float like a butterfly, sting</u>
                                         24

<u>like a bee. '</u> By adding imagery, <u>plane</u> old writing can become something more.
                       25

21 A egsiting

   B excited

   C exciting

   D Make no change

22 F Similes!

   G similes.

   H similes,

   J Make no change

23 A his

   B it

   C him

   D Make no change

24 F said I float like a butterfly, sting like a bee.

   G said (I float like a butterfly, sting like a bee).

   H said, "I float like a butterfly, sting like a bee."

   J Make no change

25 A plan

   B plain

   C plains

   D Make no change

GO ON

Name _____ Date _____

1066 Hastings Street
Sparta, WI 54656
February 14, 2011

Marcus Smith, President
Goodstuff Granola Company, Box 333
<u>Hershey Pennsylvania 17033</u>
26

Dear <u>Mr. Smith:</u>
27

    I have always been one of your most faithful customers. I love your

granola. However, I do have a complaint. The box said that it contained

raisins, almonds, and chocolate chips, but unfortunately there were <u>no</u>
    28

almonds at all. The rest of the granola was fine.

    Imagine my disappointment. I know that <u>Goodstuff granola company</u> has
    29

been in business for many <u>years but</u> I will think twice before buying one of
    30

your products again.

Regards,

Stella Amaral

26 F Hershey, Pa 17033

  G Hershey. PA 17033

  H Hershey, PA 17033

  J Make no change

27 A Mr. Smith,

  B mr. Smith:

  C Mr. smith

  D Make no change

28 F No

  G *no*

  H **no**

  J Make no change

29 A goodstuff granola company

  B Goodstuff Granola company

  C Goodstuff Granola Company

  D Make no change

30 F years: but

  G years, but

  H years; but

  J Make no change

GO ON

Name _____ Date _____

Part 3 Writing   Narrative

READ

Every day, you perform hundreds—maybe thousands—of actions. Most of them are ordinary, so you don't remember them for very long, if at all. You may even forget all about them. But some things stick in your mind. These memorable events will be with you for many years—maybe a lifetime.

THINK

Think of something you did recently that you will always remember.

Think about what made the experience unforgettable. Then think about the events that made up the experience.

WRITE

Write a narrative composition telling about something you did that you will always remember.

As you write your composition, remember to —

❏ focus on one experience—something you did that you will always remember

❏ organize your ideas in an order that makes sense, and connect the ideas with transitions

❏ develop your ideas with specific details

❏ make sure your composition is no longer than one page